D0724559

THE ART OF Mountain Biking

Other books by Robert Hurst:

The Cyclist's Manifesto

The Art of Cycling (formerly *The Art of Urban Cycling*)

Mountain Biking Colorado's San Juan Mountains

Road Biking Colorado's Front Range

The Bicycle Commuter's Pocket Guide

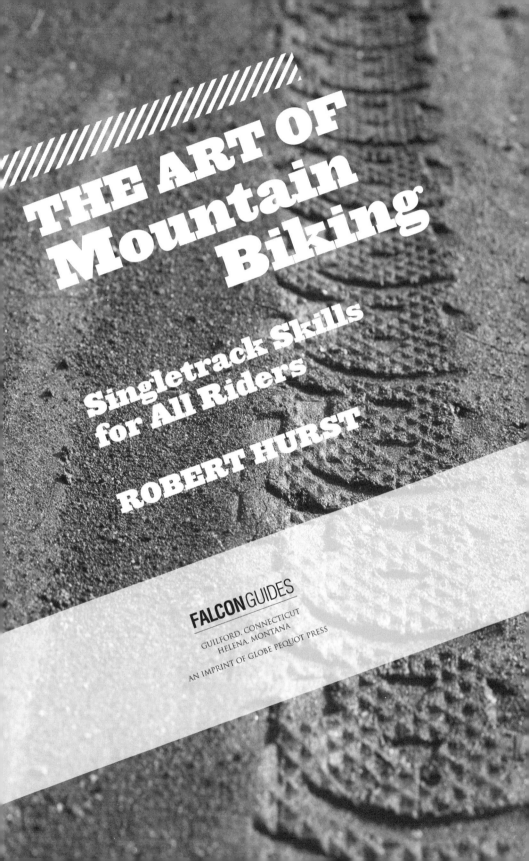

THE ART OF Mountain Biking

Singletrack Skills for All Riders

ROBERT HURST

FALCONGUIDES

GUILFORD, CONNECTICUT
HELENA, MONTANA

AN IMPRINT OF GLOBE PEQUOT PRESS

To buy books in quantity for corporate use
or incentives, call **(800) 962–0973**
or e-mail **premiums@GlobePequot.com.**

FALCONGUIDES®

FalconGuides is an imprint of Globe Pequot Press.
Falcon, FalconGuides, and Outfit Your Mind are registered trademarks of Morris Book Publishing, LLC.

Interior photos licensed by Shutterstock.com
Text design: Linda Loiewski
Layout artist: Mary Ballachino
Project editor: Gregory Hyman

Library of Congress Cataloging-in-Publication Data is available on file.

ISBN 978-0-7627-6985-8

Printed in the United States of America

10 9 8 7 6 5 4 3 2 1

For all the critters of the forest, especially the birds

CONTENTS

Part III: The Big Picture

PREFACE: WHAT THIS BOOK IS AND ISN'T

I tried to publish something here that will be useful to the beginner as well as the expert mountain biker. It is also my sincere hope that anybody who dares to read this thing will be info-tained, at least momentarily here and there, even if they've never been on a bike in their life.

The main idea behind the book is to celebrate and explain, as best I can, the art of riding a bicycle on a mountain trail, or on any singletrack trail. The book could be called *The Joy of Singletrack*. (The word "single-track," by the way, is an old railroad term, and a pejorative at that. Single-track was bad news in 1920.) Trying to get to the bottom of things, I have called upon a multitude of experienced mountain bikers, both friends and strangers, to lend their points of view on complicated and ephemeral matters of technique.

Normal trail riding (aka cross-country) features a lot of climbing. So does this book. An operative assumption of the typical cross-country rider is that climbing is a rewarding aspect of a day on the trail. If you didn't believe that, you'd always be shuttling or riding a ski lift. Lift-riding downhillers will find useful information in here but may want to avoid the climbing-related portions like they avoid climbing when out on the mountain.

This book will look at trail riding from many angles, but not from every angle. For instance, there won't be too much discussion about methods of training, and even less advice about racing. Also, this is not a good book for you if you're looking for some sort of equipment almanac to help guide your purchases, or wondering about the various clothing choices and things like that. There is not much discussion of mechanical issues or of technical aspects of equipment. We'll veer into some big-picture equipment issues occasionally, unavoidably, but the what-bike-should-I-buy stuff has been exiled to an appendix, because it can really obscure the heart of the matter.

The second and third portions of the book deal with the logistics of trail riding (e.g., what to bring along) and the big issues that are facing the sport and its somewhat uncertain future.

There's no way anybody fully understands trail riding by reading a book. I can only hope that reading this one will open your mind to some helpful ideas and have some small part in assisting your never-ending progression as a rider. "Only when it is known in the mind can the body know it; but knowing with the body is superior to knowing with the mind."[1]

INTRODUCTION: 1982

Nineteen eighty-two was not one of those terribly memorable years, which of course can be a good thing. Over at Cheyenne Mountain Junior High School, snuggled up against the piney foothills of west Colorado Springs, only a few of the kids were even slightly interested in Christopher B.'s new Specialized Stumpjumper, sparkly pewter in color, even though it was probably one of the first production mountain bikes to be locked at a bike rack at any junior high in the world. About 200 yards away from an amazing network of trails, at the dawn of the age of the mountain bike, 99.7 percent of the kids of CMJHS could not have cared less. We were getting all riled up about lacrosse back then, a new sport in Colorado. (Once we found out there was a game that allowed—no, *encouraged*—beating your opponents with a stick, all bets were off.)

It was normal for American kids to ride bikes in the early 1980s—younger kids. Once you started to grow hair in your various sensitive zones it was expected that you would move on to other things. Failing to ditch one's bicycle, in the era before the mountain bike or even Greg Lemond, was regarded with serious suspicion. There were maybe three of us in the whole school district who had any interest in riding bikes—Keith, James, and myself. When we weren't using our suburban block as a makeshift velodrome, we would ride downtown and pester the employees at Criterium Bicycle Shop, when it was on North Tejon next to Patinka's shoe repair. Hanging out in the shoebox-size shop all day, inhaling the fumes from Avocet tires and ShaverSport skinsuits, staring at posters of Joop Zoetemelk, we heard constant chatter about the new machines that people had been riding in Marin County and Crested Butte. There were rumors and excitement in the air. Legend had it that these miracle bikes were damn near indestructible (a claim we were more than happy to test when the first shipment arrived, by taking one over to the college library and jumping it off an assortment of tall ledges and stairways) and that they could negotiate impossibly steep climbs with their tiny gears, roll on water, fly . . . Almost all true.

Hiking up and down Pikes Peak about a year before the arrival of the Stumpjumpers, Keith, James, and I talked about what it might be like to ride these mythical new bikes on our familiar Front Range hiking trails. We held our arms out in front of us as we descended the Peak, gripping imaginary handlebars, launching our imaginary bikes off the big waterbar humps which seemed like they were designed especially for that purpose. If you loved bikes and being in the mountains as we did, it all seemed way too good to be true.

We had no idea. Soon, truth itself would have to be redefined.

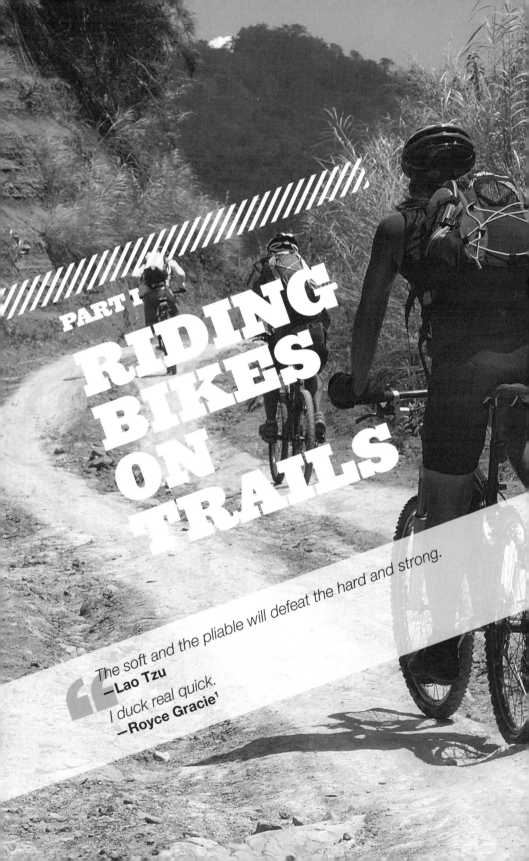

PART I

RIDING BIKES ON TRAILS

The soft and the pliable will defeat the hard and strong.
—**Lao Tzu**

I duck real quick.
—**Royce Gracie**[1]

THE SOFT STYLE Tai Chi Chuan, loosely translated "I am going to pulverize your internal organs with my supreme ultimate fist,"* is a Chinese martial art of mysterious origin. According to one school of thought, Tai Chi can be traced back to the Sung period (AD 969–1279) and the Wu-Tang Mountains, where it was developed to fend off marauding bandits.[2] In the late twentieth century, the methodical training rituals of Tai Chi were co-opted by Westerners as a New Age fitness/meditation routine, like hipster Jazzercise. These days it's common to see people lined up in parks in cities all over the world, improving their balance and core strength by performing Tai Chi's characteristic slow movements. Originally, however, Tai Chi was a highly technical method of beating an endless stream of bandits like a gong in real hand-to-hand combat. Sometimes those bandits just won't quit.

As a soft-style martial art, Tai Chi provides intricate, practiced methods of absorbing aggressive attacks, sticking to them, and manipulating the assailant's center of gravity to put him off balance. Rather than block an attempted blow, the defender feels out the energy of the move and absorbs or redirects it. The upper body is so relaxed and pliable that it gives way in response to the slightest touch.

"Drawing the opponent in so that his energy lands on nothing is a marvelous technique," Wu Ch'eng-ch'ing explained in the early nineteenth century, reflecting an ancient aphorism. "Let him attack with great force, while I deflect a thousand pounds with four ounces." Once the assailant's energy is neutralized, it's not like the Tai Chi master is going to let mister bandit off the hook. Oh no. There is tremendous power and fury stored up in that supreme ultimate fist. After absorbing the assailant's energy, it's time to dish out some of your own. "When we are attacked with great force, only softness and roundness can neutralize it; when the opponent's force is already neutralized, only hardness and straightness will repel him for a great distance."[3] When it's all said and done, the Tai Chi master has delivered a real yin-yang ass-kicking.

---

* Actually just "Supreme Ultimate Fist."

The "internal" style of martial arts, epitomized by Tai Chi, spread from China to Japan, where it developed into jujitsu and then judo. (Conversely, the Chinese "external," or hard-power, martial arts, exemplified by Shaolin kung fu, led to karate and Tae Kwon Do in Japan.) Eventually the Japanese versions of soft martial arts were introduced into Brazil, where they took on a life of their own.

The soft style came to an American audience in the 1990s, embodied in Royce Gracie, a Brazilian jiu-jitsu master. Gracie dominated the early years of the Ultimate Fighting Championship ("cage fighting"). In a string of quick fights, he submitted hard-power striking experts, burly knockout artists who had fifty or more pounds on him. Gracie's dominance proved that you didn't have to be the strongest, roughest dude or hit the hardest. The superiority of the soft style was obvious. Today every mixed martial arts fighter is a student on some level of Brazilian jiu-jitsu. Or else they get slaughtered in the ring.

Not surprisingly, the average middle-aged American sports fan is unaware that Royce Gracie ever existed, but most would instantly recognize the image of Bruce Lee. In addition to being a charismatic movie star, Lee was a top athlete and a legit expert in Shaolin kung fu, the quintessential hard-power martial art. Part of Lee's shtick was to stand there and flex all the muscles in his upper body and look very, very unrelaxed. Lee's extreme hard-power stance emerged as one of the iconic images of twentieth-century pop culture.* As awesome as Lee was, repelling legions of pajama-clad actors with fists of fury, the available evidence suggests that Gracie could have soft-powered him into submission rather quickly and unceremoniously. Lee was show business; soft power is serious business.

The principles and processes of Chinese martial arts are linked to ancient religious traditions and are consciously presented as being indistinguishable from them. This, of course, is quite different from mountain biking and other Western recreational pursuits. (Westerners like me often

---

* Somehow Lee's super-tension speaks to Americans, whereas Gracie is unknown, and the floppiness of Jackie Chan—soft-power stuff all the way—is unrecognized for its devastating martial possibilities. Chan happens to have been one of the many athletic extras hired to get brutally fended off by Lee in his movies.

speak in terms of spirituality when describing our intense outdoor experiences, but informally.) On the other hand, the essential physical basics, the fundamentals, that govern Tai Chi and many other martial arts, and with which the instructors and masters of the discipline are obsessed, are the very same fundamentals that govern the act of mountain biking, and with which the instructors and masters of mountain biking are obsessed: relaxation, balance, breathing, vision, constant movement, explosive power, endurance. It seems that we might be able to become better mountain bikers simply by studying the opening principles of Tai Chi, if the art has refined the methods of controlling these fundamentals over hundreds, if not thousands, of years.

Obviously, mountain biking and the martial arts exist for different reasons. Can the principles of a martial art translate to an activity where there is no apparent marauding bandit to fend off? Does it make any sense to view the *trail* as an opponent? It might, if it were coming at us aggressively, feinting and dodging, jabbing deadwood into our spokes like some kind of dirt ninja. It may seem so at times. If it does, that's a bad sign. Because, in fact, the trail isn't jabbing anyone or doing anything at all—you are.

WU-TANG MOUNTAIN BIKING As is common when humans are frustrated by inanimate objects, it is easy to fall into a state of antagonism with the trail, with the rocks and dirt and the earth that spawned it. In this willful state, I have often reminded myself: "Ride the trail. Don't let the trail ride you." Pretty sharp sound bite, I always thought. This kind of instruction seems to make good sense to experienced trail surfers. Beginners may find it immediately helpful. It means, choose your own line, instead of letting the features of the trail choose for you. Don't be jostled around where you don't want to go. Take control, make it happen. As one old friend of mine puts it, "Look, decide, ride."

Look. Decide. Ride. There is a lot of willful wanting and doing in that phrase. At its core—decide—it sings with yang, fire, aggression. It happens to be *helpful advice*. And it rhymes. But does "look, decide, ride" really describe what happens when we navigate a section of singletrack? The word "ride" is a possible hint. Maybe that word does not mean what we think it means. In "ride" there is both action and acceptance.

Although the trail is in some sense alive, not entirely unyielding, and changing over time (being composed of zillions of little and not-so-little shifting components), it does a decent impression of an inanimate object, or a pile of them. We see before us the geometric parameters. There is no use arguing with them. We mountain bikers can talk about willful choosing all day long if we want, and it sounds pretty good to our own ears. Ultimately, however, our range of choices is determined by the trail. We cannot force our bikes to roll anywhere we'd like, only where the geometry allows. The only thing to do is *flow* with the trail. And with this flow we are back over to the yielding yin side of things, the empty vessel, the so-called feminine energy, versus the masculine yang of "decide."

No experienced trail rider who thinks about it for a minute or two could deny that the sport involves a mysterious combination of active and passive elements. A failure to appreciate and cultivate both sides of the circle will block a mountain biker's ability to develop and improve.

The application of "soft power" is a common but often sneakily hidden feature in many areas of modern life. The term is commonly used in international relations, for instance, to describe just about any method of influence other than coercion through military force. A different kind of soft power is important in our popular sports, although it takes a backseat to hard hits and other explosive movements, and casual fans may not even notice it. Some basketball players are said to possess a "soft shooting touch." (Try shooting a basketball any other way.) Football receivers and hockey players are occasionally praised for "soft hands" amid the intense violence of those sports. Soccer players need "soft feet" to trap and control hard passes—very Tai Chi.

More so than any of these activities, and almost as much as Tai Chi itself, trail riding is inseparable from soft power. Mountain biking is one of the quintessential soft arts.

THE GOLDEN TICKET Relaxation is an interesting form of action. Paradoxical. And how can relaxation be "critical" anyway? That doesn't sound very relaxing. If relaxation is so critical, get me a huge leather chair and an umbrella drink—*stat!*

Relaxation as a foundation for successful action is a prominent recurring theme in all kinds of sporting activities, from marathon running to tiddlywinks. Rock climbing, for instance: "Relax, breathe and drift with the flow." Downhill skiing: "Relax, briefly scope your line, take a deep breath, and let your skis release onto the slope." Cross-country skiing: "One of the most important aspects of cross country skiing technique for advancing and building your skills is to *relax.*" In-line skating: "The key to becoming a successful in-line skater is developing a total sense of relaxation atop your skates." Tennis: "Relaxation produces smooth strokes." Shooting a free throw: "Use deep breathing to relax your mind and body . . . Relax your shoulders, letting them drop and loosen. Do the same for your arms, hands, and fingers." Bowling: "Keep your fingers, and especially your thumb, relaxed throughout your entire swing." Even the *hard*-power martial arts: "The very first lesson at the Kung Fu Academy, the absolute basic building block of the art, is one word: Relax." Finally, consider Jack London's advice on surfing, from an article he wrote in 1908: "The whole method of surf-riding and surf-fighting, I learned, is one of non-resistance. . . . Never be rigid. Relax." (J. L. could have said, more simply, "Hang loose.")[4] There's a lot of relaxation going on here.

Now throw some elaborate mechanical vehicles into the mix. Does the presence of such a contraption absolve the operator of this need to relax? Apparently not. Bob Bondurant to the performance driver: "If you are relaxed, you will definitely be a lot quicker." Performance motorcycling guru Keith Code equates relaxation and control: "*Take control. . . . Relax.*" Motocross pro Bryan Nylander explains why you have to let go a little bit to maintain control, just like that old .38 Special song: "Relax, let the bike float. . . . When you fight the front end over sections the bike has a tendency to throw off a rider's balance."[5] Pro motocrossers are so relaxed when they race; it's beautiful to watch. They are masters of controlled floppiness.

It's not just sports and games. "Relaxation is key," we are told, for playing the flute, stage acting, nailing job interviews, achieving orgasm, and "a more efficient labor."[6] Many of the stages of life are represented there; it's no surprise. Being tense will ruin anything and everything.

Notice that nobody ever advises anybody to prepare for action through elaborate flexing and making neck veins bulge out, Bruce Lee–style.

THE LABYRINTH Somehow, relaxation is at least as important to you, the mountain bike trail rider, as it is for any of the aforementioned jokers. Every mountain bike book worth its salt preaches the virtues of relaxation. It's an obvious bit but needs to be spewed nonetheless, because it's plain to see that beginners aren't relaxed enough. It's the first thing we notice that tags someone as a beginner. It's in the way they attach themselves to the bike. And old hands can always use a refresher on one of the most crucial aspects of the ride. We'll see over and over how relaxation is the golden ticket.

The relationship between relaxation and good mountain biking is strong and important, but it is also complex, multifaceted, and probably impossible to define. On a purely mechanical level, the importance of relaxation in trail riding is compounded by the added complexity of balancing oneself while being astride two wheels, on a dodgy surface.

The balancing and steering of bicycles (even on a perfectly smooth surface) is disturbingly complicated. At high speeds, the bicycle wants to keep itself upright to some degree, the manifestation of gyroscopic forces; turning is accomplished by leaning the bike over, and with counter-steer—that is, by turning the handlebars *away* from the turn. Road riders and motorcyclists are familiar with these phenomena (whether they realize it or not). At lower speeds common in cross-country trail riding, however, the body's system of maintaining balance has to work a lot harder, and turning the bike is not accomplished by counter-steer, just plain ol' steer.* (Negotiating a slow right-hand switchback requires turning the bars to the right; negotiating a fast right-hand curve requires turning the bars

---

* This change seems to occur when speed drops to around 6 miles per hour or lower.

to the left. Don't try to understand it, just live it.) To keep the machine on track, to stay upright, requires constant adjustment and readjustment using very small movements of the body mass, or parts of it, and minute steering motions that keep the contact patch of the front tire under the center of mass of the bike-rider system (kind of like balancing a broom upright on your palm).[7] Any six-year-old who has just learned to ride has already mastered this process. Performing these tasks on an uneven, or loose, surface ramps up the complexity by orders of magnitude, but to an experienced—relaxed—trail jockey it's still nearly effortless, unconscious.

The physiological center of human balance, as well as hearing, is buried in the inner ear, in a surreal collection of bird-bones, globes, and tubes called the labyrinth. The labyrinth includes many tiny, distinctive components—Corti's organ, the ganglion of Scarpa, and Hensen's stripe, to name a few favorites—but consists of three main parts, each of which is more bizarre than anything in a Dali painting. These parts are the semicircular canals, the shell-like cochlea, and, in between, the vestibule. Within the bony structure of the vestibule are two membranous sacs—that's right, membranous sacs—the utricle and saccule, filled with fluid and lined with hair cells, which perform much of the heavy lifting in human balance. Deep in the heart of the labyrinth, of all places, are the magic sacs that set us free.

Information about minute changes in the disposition of the fluid in the sacs—information about any movement of the head—is sent to the brain for processing.[8] With practice your brain learns better what to do with the info. A well-developed labyrinth-eyeball-processor-muscle feedback system deals with the tiniest movements and disruptions, and maintains balance by firing specific combinations of muscles with split-split-second timing, before the conscious mind knows what happened. The labyrinth is highly sensitive, very finely tuned. Asking it to perform the same function while being slammed this way and that on a rough singletrack is pretty much absurd. That it works at all on the trail is amazing. Be kind to your sacs.

On a very basic mechanical level, the whole system of human balance depends on the relaxation of the rider's muscles: When muscles are tense, locked, they can't respond properly when they receive signals from the labyrinth via the brain. Furthermore, if the muscles of the neck, back, shoulders, and arms are tensed unnecessarily, the body is transformed into a stiff board that can be waved in the breeze from the bottom edge. Any minor knock or impact on the bottom of the stiff board rings through to the top; a little movement at the bottom might translate into a lot of movement up high, sending the top edge all over the place. By relaxing the neck muscles, we allow the head and its various byzantine components to float somewhat freely—suspended—instead of being whipped around or jackhammered by every movement from below.*

This is all about basic physical relaxation, the release of unnecessary muscle tension. Relaxation, of course, is a rather mystical realm. Emotional relaxation, a state of calm, is also necessary for good trail riding. This type of relaxation is more complex, having to do with fear, confidence, experience, concentration, something I call "trail trance," and other things that are difficult or impossible to manipulate consciously. The relationship between emotional relaxation and physical relaxation is unclear; they feed back on each other in weird ways, and perhaps can't be separated at all.

CYCLES So relaxation

is important. *Got it.* Can we just make ourselves relaxed though? Isn't that wishful thinking? Cart before the horse? Yeah, pretty much. Manufacturing relaxation out of nervous tension is not a straightforward exercise. To some

> Like everyone else I sometimes get tense on the bicycle, but I notice it quickly. Then I take a deep breath and continue the right way.
>
> **—Bernard Hinault**[10]

---

* Erik Bendix, a ski instructor, offers a similar take: "Our control centers of balance and coordination are located in our heads. If a person's head won't move independently of his neck, then any activity below the head will tend to throw and jostle the head around and will detract from the head's ability to keep him accurately informed of where he is, how fast he is moving, and what direction he is going. . . . The best athletes in any sport leave their heads very calm, even in the midst of intense limb and torso activity. They are aware of their surroundings and have a flexible kind of inner quiet that is undisturbed by the chaos around them. That requires true independence between head and neck. Yet for some reason, athletic training has little language for the use of the head. Maybe that is because there isn't much muscle in the head that can be trained. The head works mainly by how its weight is balanced and by what its owner is thinking."[9] Bendix is a convert of the Alexander Technique, an established educational regime focused on the release of unnecessary tension.

degree, it is possible to relax oneself, but it will come much more easily as an organic product of the ride itself, as controlled, stylish riding feeds back into confidence, more good riding, further relaxation, etc.—the Virtuous Cycle of Trail Riding. You'll find this Virtuous Cycle very much preferable to the Cycle of Failure, which includes tension, frustration, excessive braking, and fear, and with which we old trail riders are also intimately familiar. While mountain biking, we always seem to be held in one of these two powerful spin cycles.

Simply exhorting someone to relax is rarely effective and occasionally counterproductive. "The command from someone else or from yourself to relax, often spoken as if to an idiot, only causes more tension and tightness," writes W. Timothy Gallwey, author of *The Inner Game of Tennis*, *The Inner Game of Golf*, and *The Inner Game of Writing Books With 'Inner Game' in the Title*.[11] Agreed. It won't work to scold yourself or somebody else into a state of relaxation. And maybe you shouldn't anyway. Not all nervousness should be banished or reflexively transformed into its opposite—maybe it's a signal that you've surpassed the scope of your abilities, in which case it's an important signal to heed. In those situations, the best path to relaxation is to respect the fear. Simply slow down, breathe, and reenter the zone of control. Make sure you are using your eyes properly (see page 24). Of course, if you don't push yourself a little, you'll never learn. Look for a general level of intensity that is within your grasp, with short periods of greater challenge to coax incremental improvements. This allows relaxation to emerge organically.

Various methods do exist, from the scientific to the occult, to spontaneously trick, coax, or force oneself into chilling out and releasing muscle tension. For thousands of years we've been working on this one, having recognized the importance of relaxation for both action and thought.

We can see that breath control is a common theme of ancient relaxation-seeking regimens, from Tai Chi to Indian hatha yoga. Deep, controlled breathing. Of course, it's a lot more than just that. Those breathing exercises tend to have deep spiritual and historical roots, part of comprehensive philosophies. Some of it is highly developed in a technical sense as well. When these ideas are translated through the crass commercial filter, they lose some or all of their meaning. It's fertile ground for hucksterism. I won't try to get into it too deeply here because I'd never be able to do it justice, and I would just sound like another ersatz yogi trying to recruit you for the cult. Suffice to say it may be possible to release some unwanted tension with deep, deliberate breathing, and thus hop into the Virtuous Cycle that way.

That's all we're getting into here, basic physical relaxation, nothing too mystical about it. Many very successful athletes, including Juli Furtado, one of the most dominant bike racers in history, have preached the benefits of deep, controlled breathing techniques to affect immediate real-time improvement in performance while descending. Try it and see if it works for you.

I use controlled breathing myself, but controlled posture seems to be more useful for encouraging relaxation on the trail.

THE EMPTY VESSEL It can be interesting and informative for us cyclists to observe the expert riders of horses—not necessarily their normal riding positions used while trotting or walking, which are probably a bit too upright for our purposes, but the position assumed by the rider on a galloping or jumping animal. It's kind of a radical position and,

> Floatation is groovy . . .
> —**Jimi Hendrix, "Power to Love"**

at the same time, completely natural. Notice there is *no sitting* going on at that point, and *no standing* either. The rear is entirely off the saddle, but it's still low. The legs are as bent as they can reasonably be, pumping up and down with the horse. The arms are very bent as well, with the forearms very low, and moving back and forth with the beast's bobbing head. The arms and legs are the only parts of the rider's body making any serious movement. Head is up and eyes are forward. In this position—and only in this position—the jockey is almost immune to the radical gyrations of a very excited 1,000-pound beast attached to his feet.

Although there are some differences, the jockey's position has very much in common with the proper mountain biking position for rough terrain, or descending fast. The same basic principles apply. The rear end is off the seat, so when the beast pops up the rider doesn't pop up with it. The arms and legs are very bent and flex or extend as the bike rocks and rolls, while the head and upper body remain more or less level and calm. The inner thighs lightly touch or brace against the saddle to steady the bike and the body in interesting ways. The weight is on the feet, primarily, but the center of gravity is not quite where it would be if the rider were simply standing up on the pedals. It's more like a crouch. In this crouch the rider appears ready to spring upward—in fact, they *are* ready to spring upward if necessary (occasionally it is), but that's not what it's all about. Racing legend Ned Overend calls this the "attack position."[12] While we can see what he's getting at, his aggressive formulation seems to discard the critical soft-power aspects of the technique.

While a horse weighs massively more than its rider, the cyclist weighs massively more than the bike. Thank you, Captain Obvious. But think for a moment about the significance of this obviousness. This means that movements of the rider's mass can profoundly affect the bike-rider system—the cyclist's mass dominates the bike. Good trail riders understand this very well, and enjoy crawling all over their machines, throwing their weight far forward and back, to the sides, using exaggerated body movements to ease their rigs around corners and over obstacles. This is definitely something that beginners should practice. One learns immediately that the prerequisite for this sort of movement is to be off the saddle, and physically loose.

A very relaxed, detached position lets the rider shift position easily, quickly, and quite radically if necessary, anticipating severe twists or vertical features in the favored line. In a fluid position over the bike, the rider can weight or unweight either wheel separately, or at once, to great effect. Riders who are radically relaxed can afford these helpful, exaggerated shifts in body weight, out of center, while tense riders must remain directly over the bike all the time to keep rolling. A profoundly relaxed rider can even get surprised and knocked way off-kilter by the trail and regain control seamlessly.

Looking deeper into this crouching off-the-saddle position, however, it's clear that its main purpose is not so much to allow the rider to move, but to let the body remain relatively *still* as the bike moves, or is moved, under it. Suspension: a body separated from the saddle and supported only on supple, bent limbs, like the jockey on a galloping horse, is poised to absorb any upward movement of the machine, and all the rough stuff, without letting it transfer straight through to the skull. And a rider in this absorbent crouch is also ready to actively pull the bike upward into the body, and ready to push it away to match the terrain. Push, pull. Absorb, accept. Yin, yang. It is a *centered* position, from which the rider can move in any direction relative to the machine, even down. It is a position out of which the rider can be moved or knocked in any direction and still maintain control. More importantly, it is a position from which the bike can be manipulated, directed up, down, or to the sides, to follow smooth lines or smooth out rough ones.

We are left with another trail paradox: The mountain biker must achieve independence from the bicycle in order to "become one" with it.

By no means should the cyclist be in this crouching tiger, ready position all the time. Most of the time spent riding trails will be spent climbing. The lower speeds, tamer impacts, and the necessities of traction and power transfer all dictate a different optimal position for climbing. (More on that in a bit.) And obviously you don't need to be crouched over the bike in the ready position whenever you're not climbing. There are times when you can just roll along, perched on the seat in a more-or-less sitting position, conserving energy. Even while "sitting," however, the trail rider should feel light, ready to move. The crouching ready position should never be more than a tiny unconscious flick of the rear end away.

One of the big pitfalls of trail riding is to become too enamored with the full sitting position, especially in the later stages of a ride. As fatigue sets in, the body's mass grows heavy. It seems more and more of a chore to lift it even a little, and failing to do so makes getting over obstacles even more difficult and fatiguing. Thus the rider enters a negative feedback loop of disintegrating technique and ride quality. Avoid that by consciously willing your arse off the saddle, just a little, when it starts to feel heavy. Think about changing position regularly on a long seated climb, even from one type of seated position to another, or else one specific combo of muscles is going to get burned.

Any discussion of position—of any aspect of off-road technique, really—is complicated by the existence of a wide range of different bicycle suspension systems. Those with extra-cushy setups may be better off sitting at times when others are out of the saddle. Nobody fully understands what's going on there. Different bikes, different riders, different days, different everything. You'll just have to ride a lot and get to know your bike, whatever kind of bike it is.

STRANGE CARGO It seems likely that a perfectly designed mountain biking body would be set up very differently than the typical human form. Maybe there would be no head at all, for instance. The brain, labyrinth, and other critical pieces-parts would be located somewhere lower down, like the middle of the chest. Maybe the eyes would be on long flexible stalks protruding from the top of the torso. Now that you've got that disturbing image in your mind, ask yourself, is the actual human form any less of a freak show? We've got these crazy Tootsie Pops lolling around up there all the time. It's no less weird, and it can complicate the trail riding.

> QUESTION: What's more fun than a barrelful of monkeys?
>
> ANSWER: An alien with a big pop-off head!
>
> —**From an advertisement for Big Head dog toys**[13]

Despite the presence of several bizarrely adorned orifices, the adult human head can easily weigh about half as much as a typical cross-country bike. Think about the weight of at least three Mavic Crossmax ST wheel sets (six wheels)* on top of your neck.

Having that bowling ball up there is actually a stabilizing force much of the time. But when it's waving around, at the highest point of the bike-rider system, sloshing back and forth maniacally, or just sitting in the

---

* About 1,600 grams per set.

wrong spot, it causes serious balance and control issues. Even if our precious membranous sacs of the inner ear remain calm and function perfectly, a misplaced or rogue noggin will cause a dismount.

The weight of the head is always something of a factor for the trail rider, and especially so when the slope points sharply uphill. When the rider's mass, led by the head, moves too far back on a steep climb, the front wheel unweights, breaks traction, even levitates above the dirt. Advanced riders intentionally work this point of balance to ease their front wheel onto ledges and over rocks while climbing—a lot easier than pulling up with the muscles. The beginner wants nothing more than to escape it, but can't, feels persecuted, and slips into a minor panic. With each pedal stroke the bars are wrenched in desperation, the front tire flips back and forth. The bike meanders, uncontrolled. The rider clips out, stymied. These front wheel shenanigans are a common frustration when learning to climb steep hills. I think you'll agree, no matter what skill level you've reached on the bike. As experts, we remember it. As beginners, we're living it.

Beyond learning to love that feeling of weightlessness, it must be controlled. To control the front wheel, one must first control the weight of the head. Slide forward on the seat and consciously lower the back, neck, and head together. Think about bringing the chin down toward the stem. You might want to flare the elbows out a bit or put them down below the bars to help pull the bike down. However you can control the head and keep the upper body low enough to climb steep trails comfortably, front wheel under control, consider this your Extreme Climbing Position. It is the opposite of the Extreme Descending Position, in which the arse is off the seat and behind it. You'll be floating around somewhere between these two extremes at all times, depending on the terrain and what you want to do with it (or, what it wants to do with you).

There is a sweet spot for almost any steep climb, an equilibrium, in which the weight of the head is low enough to keep the front wheel on track, and the rear is far enough back to maintain traction below the drive tire. Those who have more trouble finding traction for the rear than controlling the front may simply need to scoot back a little more, redistribute the weight. Conversely, if rear traction is no problem at all (on slickrock or granite, for instance), one can get off the seat and way out over the front of the bike. Weight distribution is a critical issue for steep climbs, but hardly the only one. Many factors come into play and any one of them can cause a total short circuit: Cadence, power transfer, vision, and line choice are all extremely important.

A CAUTIONARY NOTE ON SUSPEN-SION
Obviously, the suspension components of the bike are there to perform the shock-absorbing function I have just described for arms and legs. Should the biological suspension prove inadequate, the shocks will be there. Ideally a rider will use the mechanical suspension as a supplement to proper soft-power body English, and will be able to ride faster and easier using both suspension systems than would be possible using just one or the other. A potential concern arises, however, that the mechanical suspension might simply fill in for what the novice lacks in the way of posture and relaxation, allowing that rider to continue navigating trails at some minimum level without correcting those basic mistakes. In this way, suspension technology could act like a crutch that prevents one's learning to walk.

One of the people I ride with has never really learned, despite her many years of off-road cycling, to lift the front wheel off the ground.* For some reason this otherwise super-strong and smooth rider never became comfortable with the basic action of manipulating her body mass to unweight the front wheel. From the beginning she has been dependent on technology to perform the soft-power function that her body can't.

---

* For the sake of simplicity, I'm going to label any lifting of the front wheel, no matter how small, a "wheelie." But there are distinctly different ways to lift the front wheel. For instance, one could lift the wheel while coasting, a maneuver known as a "manual." Or one could use a pedal stroke to aid the lifting of the wheel. Those of us who grew up riding in the '70s and '80s tend to think of a wheelie as something much more impressive than merely lifting the wheel—to ride a real wheelie you have to keep the front off the ground for some notable distance, like halfway down the block, from Chris's house to Chuck's driveway. In any case, the lifting can be initiated and controlled almost entirely by moving the body weight, and need not involve much upward yanking on the bars. A lot of beginners assume the wheelie comes from yanking on the bars, but to yank on the bars the rider must hunch over the front of the bike. Only the quickest wheelie is possible while hunching over the front of the bike. To get the feel of it, shift your mountain bike into the granny gear on flat ground. Then, while seated, hammer the pedals from a stop. You'll feel the front of the bike trying to pop right into the air, without any upward pulling on the bars, not unlike a drag racer taking off from the line, rearing up on the back tires.

In practical terms, this means that whenever she encounters a big root or rock in the singletrack one of three things happens: (1) she bangs into the obstacle and rolls over it due to the magical properties of her Fox RL32; (2) she stops dead in her tracks, gets off the bike, and carries it over; or (3) she T-bones the object, bounces straight up in the air, and clips out just in time while letting out a startled yelp. The first option is, at best, satisfactory. The remaining two are pretty terrible, compared to the way it should be. This is a rider who would have been better off learning basic trail skills on a rigid fork.

HANDS On the aforementioned steep climbs, the hands can be recruited to apply a little extra downward force all the way to the backside of the bike, simply by twisting the grips backward along with each pedal stroke. This nifty old trick results in a noticeable increase in traction to the rear tire. The grips can also be twisted the other direction and pushed forward when the front tire is in the air, which helps bring the rear end off the ground (the "bunny hop"). Take a look at the forearms of expert trail riders. They're ripped, which shows that there's a lot of spirited handlebar manipulation going on.

> You don't need to break an egg to score a goal.
> —**Ancient soccer wisdom**

In general, however, trail riders should strive for a light touch on the grips ("soft hands"), especially while climbing. In overly simple terms, one should hold the bars only as firmly as necessary to maintain control and manipulate the front end where needed, and no more firmly than that. (If you don't need the extra traction from twisting the grips, don't do it.) In reality, there will be moments of panicked grabbing and desperate yanking, all part of the game. Everybody reverts to that on occasion. (In order to deal with these clumsier moments, add endurance to the whole upper-body muscle complex, and protect the hands during unscheduled dismounts, savvy off-roaders use full-fingered gloves.)

Dropping below the minimum grip energy is fraught with peril, of course, as the bars can be ripped away when the front wheel twists against something, or just bounced casually out of the hands due to a minor bump.

Still, holding on too tight is the more common pitfall and a more perni-cious problem. A death grip on the handlebars is both a symptom and a cause of poor trail mojo—part of the Cycle of Failure. When in doubt, relax. We've already discussed how a stiff upper body can ruin a finely tuned system of balance. Relaxing the grip is a good first step to relaxing the forearms, upper arms, shoulders, and neck.

If you are freaked out by the notion of a light grip on the bars, and have trouble understanding how it relates to traditional notions of manual control, consider the common bowling tip, to relax the grip all the way through the swing. The bowler is advised to hold the ball as loosely as it can be held—while he or she hauls back and hurls the thing with serious velocity into the pins.[14] Relax the grip? Seems a bit insane, to the uniniti-ated. But really it's the only way the hand can finesse the ball onto the right path—the soft-power stuff. Only a tiny amount of muscle tension is needed to actually hold and direct the ball; the rest is messing up the pro-gram, sending it toward the gutter. The same basic idea goes for holding onto the trail bike.

One of my more unconventional friends has been preaching for years about a trick he calls "Angel Wing Technology," which he uses when climbing tough hills. He simply means that he consciously relaxes his hands and the rest of the muscles of his upper body as much as they can be relaxed while still keeping the bike upright and moving up the hill. "An absurd level of relaxation in the upper body," he says. This is com-mon advice, taken to an extreme. Often the rider will have to shift position subtly just to allow such complete relaxation, which in itself is instruc-tive. With these muscles at minimum flex, the only muscles left working are those that are absolutely necessary to propel the bike upward. These include muscle groups in the abdomen and lower back as well as the legs and butt.

Using this soft-power strategy, one can actually feel the energy that had been locked uselessly in the hands, arms, and upper torso flow into the lower half, where it is most welcome and put to immediate use. Ned Overend notes, "When you remember to relax your neck and shoulders while climbing . . . the whole body benefits." Describing his seated climb-ing position, road racing great Bernard Hinault says, "I avoid holding on too tightly with the fingers because I strive to avoid all useless tension. Relaxed shoulders, arms and hands are very important . . . Even when I climb out of the saddle I try to be as relaxed as possible."[15]

The physical sensation of extra energy arriving on the scene is psychologically powerful. Combined with the resulting lightness in the shoulders and upper back, it feels a bit like a set of wings has been installed. "Angel Wing Technology" has the added benefit of eliminating all that unwanted yanking of the bars on steep slopes (see pages 15 and 56), which, if smooth lines are available and the rider is adept at finding them, allows him or her to sit more upright and further back on the saddle for greater traction.

NOTES ON BIKE SETUP AND FIT

For cross-country trail riding, the placement of the handlebars and grips should facilitate a riding position that is not too far from the casual road-riding position, in which the hands are "on the tops" or near the brake hoods, or somewhere in between. In other words, the triangle formed by the contact points (grips, pedals, and saddle) should be roughly similar to the triangle formed by the pedals, saddle, and the curve at the top of your road handlebars, if you've got a road bike and it happens to be set up comfortably. That's one man's opinion, anyway, about setting up bikes that will spend a lot time going up as well as down. Without any such template, the setup of the mountain bike will have to be improvised even more than the usual crapshoot.

The first step to fitting a mountain bike is to make sure there will be plenty of stand-over height so that the top tube doesn't mangle your crotch every time you try to put a foot on the ground. This has emerged as a more common issue with the use of "700c" (29-inch) wheels on trail bikes, which tends to raise the top tube. For mountain bikers, insufficient stand-over clearance is a deal-breaker. Cure for insufficient stand-over: Get a different frame, or longer legs.

I'm going to assume from here that the frame fits reasonably well, with enough stand-over and a decent top tube length. In which case, the next thing to do is set the proper seat height. When pedaling, the leg should be slightly bent when the pedal is at six o'clock with ankle flat. You shouldn't have to reach or rock the hips at all to reach the bottom of the pedal stroke. Pedaling hard with a too-high saddle will badly mess with the hips and knees, quickly causing damage. Set it too low and you might ruin the knees anyway. Note that the low seat position favored by downhillers and other gravity racers is not proper for cross-country riding. Use the same seat height you'd use for riding on the road.

Back in the Day people loved using low seat height for descending but wanted regular height for climbing, so the bikes had quick-release seat posts that allowed riders to move the seat up and down during the ride. A little accessory called a Hite-Rite was popular, a spring mechanism that attached to the seat post and automatically sent it back to the proper height when the quick release was opened. At some point in the '90s, cross-country riders basically gave up on the whole concept of lowering their saddles for descents, at least around here. Now we just set our saddles at the correct height and deal with it. The gravity hounds still jam their seats into their frames.

Those looking for a more grounded method of setting seat height might try this traditional formula, which has been used by racers for decades: Measure the inseam as accurately as possible and multiply by 0.885. Many old-schoolers will tell you that this formula provides the proper distance from the center of the bottom bracket to the top of the seat.

Cleats should be set so the shoe is basically "straight" (shoes and feet themselves aren't straight in any traditional sense) when it's locked in the pedal; although individuals may prefer a little toe-in or toe-out, don't overdo that. And the ball of the foot should be, roughly, just slightly behind the pedal spindle, with some variation possible there as well. You may have to readjust cleat position after a ride or two, as personal ergonomic preferences emerge. With the cranks level, a hypothetical plumb line dropped from the knee should fall roughly at the pedal axle. So they say. I've never checked mine.

Beyond these few parameters, things get much more foggy: saddle fore-aft and tilt, handlebar height, and stem length. Contrary to majority opinion on these matters, I like somewhat low bars and a slightly downward-pointed saddle. Common advice is to keep the saddle level, but

I enjoy how my slightly forward and downward-pointed saddle turns level when the bike points up, like the benches of an incline railway. This makes steep climbs a little easier to handle. However you set up these variables, make sure they promote the physically loose riding position described earlier in the book (see page 7), as well as a comfortable climbing position. You should feel very at-home up there, shifting easily between a seated climbing position and the suspended over-the-bike position.

There is no real science to bike fit and setup (beware of bike shop guys who insist there is). What we have are superstitions that have been repeated so long that they have taken on an air of scientific truth. At the same time, small changes in the position and angles of these contact points *will* have a profound effect on the feel of the bike—pedaling efficiency, handling, and other things. Even though it's all soaked in superstition, you can't afford to take any of it lightly. Model the setups of more experienced riders whose riding styles you'd like to emulate, then use trial and error to determine which trade-offs work best for you.

The trend toward longer and longer shocks and riser handlebars has raised typical hand positions several inches higher than they were in previous decades. This is the triumph of downhill/freeride bias among a new generation of riders and marketers, and a manifestation of the fact that beginners tend to be attracted to more upright positions. A shop will build the same bike today with a much higher hand position than they would have ten or fifteen years ago. Those tall front ends can feel mighty solid on descents. That's a wonderful thing, but just remember that there is no free lunch. Trade-offs, always. A downhill-oriented bike with long-travel forks and high bars will be more difficult to handle on steep climbs, simply due to its being so tall in front. Cornering will also be affected.

In addition to the position of the handlebars, pay close attention to the angle of the brake levers. They should be installed in a position that is comfortable and easy to reach from that crouching tiger-jockey stance we were discussing before, the ready-for-action position. That's the position you'll likely be hovering around when you need to use the brakes. Make sure the levers aren't pointed down too much, as you'll have to reach over the bars to get at them. A good rule of thumb is that they should be placed at the same angle as the forearms, and then twisted upward a smidgeon. Think about placing them so that the angle of the wrist is a little flatter than the forearms. This will enable the natural suspension in the wrist instead of locking it out straight.

FEET A surprising, some might say disturbing, amount of the action in trail riding occurs at very slow speed, or no speed. And included in that term "action" would be all the various forms of toppling over and flailing around like a flipped-over cockroach. Quite often such unwanted low-speed action revolves around a dysfunctional relationship with the pedals. Beginners consume themselves with pedal unease.

The act of pulling a cleat out of a clipless pedal* often occurs in the midst of a minor panic at slow speed. While trying to get through a tricky rock garden or entering a switchback, the mind gives in, or takes over (see page 60). *I'm not going to make it* is the thought, although it might flash through faster than it can be verbalized. Such a thought, if you're having it, is almost always correct. Survival instinct takes over, and in this case "survival" means putting a foot on solid ground before toppling over awkwardly. But to step on the ground, first you've got to extract a damn foot from a pedal.

Entering a technical section, the timid novice has already tensed all the muscles on one side in anticipation of pulling out of the pedal quickly; of course, this tension alone means it will be some kind of miracle if he doesn't have to pull out of the pedal quickly. As usual, the fate of the unrelaxed rider is preordained. Instead of finding a way through the rocks, he's looking for a place to put a foot down. When the mind's attention makes that instantaneous shift from looking for a way past an obstacle to finding a landing zone beside it, that's when trail riding ends and crashing begins.

---

* A note for the uninitiated: "Clipless" pedal-cleat systems are designed to hold the cleat firmly in the pedal mechanism unless the rider performs a specific exaggerated movement with the ankle, in which case the cleat is released with an audible click. The term "clipless" refers to the old-school toe clips that mountain bikers used in the 1980s, before clipless pedal systems took over. Using clipless pedals, the rider can "clip in" or "clip out," which makes no sense. Clipless pedals have been around since the early days of bicycling but only became mainstream with the mountain bike.

Frantically, still prior to any clear thought, the ankle is trying to twist the cleat out of the pedal. But there's a catch (literally): The release mechanism only works at the correct angle. If the bike has been jostled to an awkward angle at that moment, as often happens, the panicked ankle might only succeed in pulling the bike even further toward the ground. This is one of the cruelest and most direct examples of self-fulfilling prophecy in the sport—the rider panics about falling over and thus yanks himself over.

Pedal panic is a powerful negative force that can literally ruin a ride. If your mind is on your feet, it's not where it needs to be. For any kind of improvement or success to occur, this corrosive and dysfunctional pedal-rider relationship, mired in mistrust, must end. The solution is not to switch to flat pedals, or to remove the pedals altogether, as tempting as that might sound. The solution is practice, time, and familiarity with the equipment, which breeds real confidence and relaxation. The Virtuous Cycle. Beginners may find it hard to believe, but eventually the trail rider achieves an unconscious relationship with the pedals, wherein the mechanical process of clipping in, clipping out never troubles the mind. Ideally we won't look at our pedals or think about them at all except for maintenance purposes—we forget all about them.

On a recent late-fall ride I had a chance to watch a friend climbing up a steep, rocky section of trail in front of me. In a sense, I was able to watch his unconscious mind in action; it was evident in the way he dealt with his feet. He was picking his way ever so deliberately up the singletrack, placing his tires and timing his pedal strokes just so. Ahead of a particularly vexing pile of mangled rock, over which there appeared to be no workable lines, he surveyed the scene; picking a route, he caressed his tires up through the mess. Near the top, the rear tire spit out a baseball-size chunk of granite and spun in place. These things happen. My friend didn't freak out and yank himself to the ground in response to the setback. The spin-out simply left him balanced on the bike, upright but going nowhere. Completely relaxed, he continued looking around to see if there was any sort of escape route that he could ride out of from zero mph. Finding none, he calmly located a spot to put his foot down and clipped out, a full three or four seconds after his spin-out. The whole scene was as calming as a hot cup of Sleepytime tea.

Even though this fellow's a great technical rider, he can't ride everything he comes across. But his version of not riding something is a lot smoother than most people's. There's no panic involved. Even his failed attempts to ride technical sections are relaxed and controlled, a situation which is dependent in large part on his unconscious familiarity with the pedals.

TOPPLING OVER Toppling over happens a lot more often than high-speed crashes. It can be a real problem if the landing zone is composed of jagged rocks or spiky deadwood.

If you find yourself toppling over at zero mph, try to minimize the impact with the ground by using your hand and arm as a spring; in other words, look down, reach for the ground, and ease yourself down if at all possible. (Prepare for this move with the old classic exercise, the push-up.) Done poorly—that is, with a stiff arm, a blind stab—this method can result in a broken wrist or collarbone. A disturbing number of authors advise crashing cyclists to tuck their arms in and lead with the shoulder, the idea being to save those arms and collarbones, apparently at any cost. Some even say you should just deathgrip the bars all the way into the ground. In reality, toppling over without attempting to break the fall is far more likely to result in a head injury, and just might snap the collarbone anyway.

It's the head injury that you want to avoid, first and foremost. In a lateral slow-motion crash, try to relax, look what's down there, then do what you can to make things as painless as possible—don't just close your eyes and hope for the best. Try to find a soft landing, if there is one. Learn to use the outside of the hand and forearm to initiate a softening roll. If no roll is possible, it's still a lot better to slap an arm into the ground than a head. It's a lot better to tear up a shoulder than a neck.

EYES When you first start riding trails, there is confusion about what exactly you're supposed to do with the eyes. I mean, do you just look out ahead and sort of take it all in? Are you supposed to focus on specific objects or areas of the trail? If so, which ones?

It seems silly on paper: If you don't know *why* you are looking, it will be difficult to do it well. On the trail things are happening so quickly, riders can get overwhelmed with inputs if they don't know exactly what they are looking for and where to look for it. The visible field becomes a jumbled blur, the bike an unguided missile and the rider a mere passenger upon it. This is out-of-balance riding, all yin and no yang. Not soft power—just soft. Proper use of vision is the first step toward reintroducing a necessary measure of control.

It can help a great deal to break down the process of looking into its basic components, and work backward from the desired outcome to see how vision helps us achieve it. What do we hope to accomplish with our vision? What are we really doing with it to achieve that goal? Whether the goal is to ride faster, smoother, or just safely and consistently, the successful trail rider uses vision primarily in this specific way: *looking for rideable lines.* Note—not looking for obstacles, and unrideable lines. There are plenty of those, and they are easy to find, but finding them won't help you plan a path that will actually work; in fact, it will make it more difficult or impossible to do so (see page 60). *With your eyes you are finding and choosing a path that works.*

WHAT THE GURU ON THE TOP OF THE MOUNTAIN SAYS WHEN YOU GO UP INTO HIS GURU AREA In the late

'60s young Westerners in considerable numbers went east to consult with various gurus, yogis, and wise men, many of whom were of a dubious nature. Strangely, this activity seemed to coincide with the exploding popularity of bong hits, acid trips, and other mind-expanding innovations among a restless and spiritually deprived population. (The guru-seeking path was one most famously traveled by the Beatles, after the release of *Sergeant Pepper's* but before the *White Album*.) "Oh master," the deprived Westerners pleaded, "we have come a great distance, and we are high out of our gourds. What is the meaning of life?" The yogi dispenses some very gentle words about mortality and the true nature of peace, wheezing profoundly. Later on everyone wonders if his advice was just part of an elaborate scheme to neutralize potential competition for his thriving import/export business. Also, the guru turns out to be all hands around the ladies.

Guru-visiting seems to have faded, like macramé, into the annals of history. But, it happens there is still a mountain biking guru who resides in an ancient Anasazi tomb in the rocks northwest of Durango, Colorado. He looks like ZZ Top and smells like Cheez-Its, in the style of the old masters. His calves are freakishly defined. And there is no funny business when you go to his cave, just profound advice about mountain biking.

All the things I've written about so far are a bit too obvious to make decent guru advice. All that jive about relaxation and balance, too basic. Soft power? Old news. Our MTB guru has something a lot better than that to give, one piece of advice which, like no other, will unravel the murky secrets of trail riding. Knowledge of this single, deceivingly simple secret will turn an adequate trail jockey into a really, really good one.

"Look far ahead," he says. *Look far ahead.* "And now, please leave me in peace, for tomorrow I have a long ride planned with several members of the Fort Lewis College women's team."

Look far ahead. Three words, that's it. Blink and you missed it.

Look far ahead, meaning lift your head and point your eyeballs a good distance ahead, not down at the ground. Focus not where your tires are rolling *now*, but always where you are headed *next*. The natural inclination is to stare down at the area just in front of the front wheel, for obvious reasons. That's just another way *natural inclination* can sting an off-road cyclist. The proper distance to look ahead almost always seems too far to the beginning rider, so the guru advice to beginners is: Look where you think you should be looking, then consciously lift your eyes and look a bit farther. Or a lot farther. Always. (One could almost say look up the trail as far as you can at any given point, but that's a bit much.)* Instantly, this will unlock a whole new level in your riding experience, making everything easier. It won't just make it *seem* easier, it will actually *be* much easier. Look up the trail and suddenly you will be able to ride faster and smoother, with more confidence. You'll be able to keep up with people who had been

---

* In real-world situations, this distance seems to hover in the range of 20 to 30 feet, a value that is confirmed fairly commonly by expert riders. For instance, Canadian Olympian Geoff Kabush: "It's hard to put a number on it, but I'd say I look ahead 20 or 30 feet, and never down at my wheels."[16]

leaving you in the dust. Primarily, this is because, by surveying sections of trail earlier, you have given yourself more *time* to find a good line and think about what exactly you need to do to roll it. This applies as much to slow technical climbs as it does to fast descents.

I neglected to share this tidbit with some of my riding buddies after I learned it. Selfish? Heck yeah. Don't judge. I need every advantage I can get, to avoid getting completely dusted, then laughed at. Anyway, now it's in the book, so the jig is up. I fear by divulging this information I may have put a fine guru out of a job.

Well, that's it. *Look far ahead.* That's the big guru secret. Feel free to tell your riding partners, or not.

TRAIL VISION So, we're looking well ahead, identifying potential lines and choosing them, and, of course, physically handling the bike and our bodies in order to achieve that path. Think of the trail as a partner in this endeavor, not a foe to be slashed and pummeled. The trail helpfully provides far more information than we need to ride it well. It's up to us to receive this info with our various senses, particularly the eyes.

The eyes must always be a few beats ahead of the bike. That's another way of phrasing the guru's secret from the preceding section. Keep the eyes up and always look forward to the next feature, and beyond the next feature. A little bit of looking down is inevitable and okay, but don't let the eyes linger, stuck on particular obstacles and lines. Even experienced riders need to consciously and repeatedly remind themselves to direct eyes forward. The front wheel gets jealous when you pay any attention elsewhere and shamelessly flashes its knobs to get you to look down. It should take only a tiny moment, if that, to check the progress of the front wheel and confirm that everything is proper. Any longer and you're approaching the realm of hazard fixation (see page 60) and likely to rollick off line.

It's worth reiterating the point: If any single problem consumes too much attention or takes too much time to figure out, the bike-and-rider will roll on to the next section without a plan, and the rider will be trying to solve new problems on the spot, too late, as the front tire rams into whatever happens to be there. As slow as it goes, the bike is not waiting for your brain.

Meanwhile, as you are choosing your path ahead, what else is really going on here? You are riding the lines that you chose previously—blindly. Remember that the terrain directly under the bike, beneath the tires, is impossible to see, no matter how hard we look for it. (Unless, of course, you are blessed with X-ray vision and can see right through the tire and rim.) The actual interface of bike and trail occurs in a relatively tiny area of tire-dirt contact, and it is impossible to monitor this area visually. All the actual bike-to-trail action is *felt* (through the arms and legs) rather than seen. It can be no other way.* In some sense this terrain under your tires has already been pre-ridden, by the eyes. So when you get to it, a lot of the work of riding over or around any obstacles there has already been done.

Obviously, the eyes don't need to be fixed directly on an object for your brain to identify it. For familiar things, like rocks, trees, and trail edges, they need only flash through the corner of the field of vision to be picked up and cataloged by the mind. Mountain bikers are concerned primarily with the narrow strip of real estate stretched out in front of them, vertically through the field of vision; this puts a new twist on the concept of peripheral vision—up and down instead of side to side. An extra long (rather than wide) field of vision is helpful for trail riding, as it allows a rider to take visual inventory of a long length of trail without having to move the head up or down. A helmet visor or hat brim could slip down and block the top of your trail vision, causing serious problems at high speeds.

Close-quarters fine-tuning adjustment of the front tire is possible while the primary vision is directed up-trail, and happens not quite in total blindness, but "at the bottom of the eyes," as one friend puts it. You might be able to enhance this type of trail vision with some exercises in your daily life, like trying to watch TV by looking at the wall above the set. A lot of important trail vision happens in the margins, outside the area of direct focus.

Some riders say they "just see everything" while looking at the trail, a reference to this gathering of information from the whole field of vision

---

* Without direct visual information, signals from the arms and legs, the ears, the labyrinth, and the memory conspire to keep the bike upright. To prove this beyond a shadow of a doubt, try this instructive drill: While cruising slowly on a wide piece of trail or a four-wheel-drive road, confirm that no other trail users or SUVs are approaching, then close your eyes. You'll notice that, despite the roughness of the ground below, there is no real problem riding off-road on feel alone, without any visual cues. At least, there shouldn't be. As long as you are relaxed, the inner ear's system of balance will take care of business.

while focused on a distant spot ahead. It's a familiar concept but a misunderstood one if it is imagined by the rider that he or she can just prop the face forward, point the eyes anywhere ahead, and somehow take in all relevant information. That would be more elegant than the way it really works. In reality, the eyes must sort of dart around from one spot to another.

At speed, the rider points the eyes far ahead like the guru said, consciously looking beyond to the next feature or turn. But the eyes aren't pointed intractably forward at all times. In fact, they also move downward from that position repeatedly, fixing on the line around certain features located in the area between the down-trail center of attention and the front tire. Repeatedly the eyes retreat from their primary distant focus, tracking backward toward the rider at just the right pace to *freeze the trail*—then they flick back up to the top and track down toward the rider, over and over. These quick eye movements are necessary to keep the trail from becoming an unreadable blur. It's important to realize that the eyes must continually flicker and sweep both directions, toward the rider and away, as long as the bike is moving.

The eyes function in (at least) two ways for the mountain biker: They move quickly in sharp focus between individual objects and locations, while simultaneously providing a general, somewhat vague survey of a very broad scene around these primary points of focus. We may as well label these *direct vision* and *indirect vision*.*

Effective use of vision, as much as power or balance, separates the smooth trail rider from the hack who gets knocked off the bike every few minutes.

A TALE OF TWO LINES: FRONT Up to
this point in the book we've been referring to the "line," a common term for the path that you choose for your bike. This has been quite misleading.

---

* This is similar to the medical lexicon, in which "indirect vision" is synonymous with peripheral vision, or "vision resulting from retinal stimulation beyond the macula."[17] The macula is the spot in the center of the retina where the vision is most focused. "Macula" is also the term used to describe the sensory receptors in the membranous sacs of the labyrinth, collectively (see page 7). If you're a dentist, "indirect vision" is what you use to look at and work on the backsides of people's teeth—a mirror.

Sorry. In fact, there are two lines—one for each tire—and this is actually very important to realize.

It's commonly understood by anyone who's ever ridden a bike through a puddle and looked back at the tire tracks that the front and rear wheels take wildly divergent paths when a bike is turning or weaving around. This fact holds limited importance for road cyclists and so escapes much serious consideration. With higher speeds on the road and little if any slow-speed technical maneuvering, a road cyclist can get away with ignoring the difference between the two lines. However, on the singletrack, a relatively narrow surface loaded with rocks and other vertical features, the two-line reality comes into play very often. Occasionally it causes special problems that must be overcome; at other times it can be used to special advantage.

Most new riders have enough trouble recognizing and dealing with the single-line concept. They have to come to terms with that before we introduce a new layer of complexity. Learning to "take care of the front wheel" comes first.

When choosing a line for the front tire, see the trail and potential lines in all their three-dimensional glory. The singletrack can only rarely be described as a flat surface or a flat surface with a scattering of obstacles to be steered around. This means available lines are rarely flat, two-dimensional. They go up and down as well as side to side, and usually a little bit of both at the same time.

We are finding these lines, not creating them. Perhaps "line recognition" is the best term to describe what the mountain biker is really doing out there.

When I first began to carve I fixed my gaze upon the animal in front of me. After three years I no longer saw it as a whole bull, but as a thing already divided into parts. Nowadays I no longer see it with the eye; I merely apprehend it with the soul. My sense-organs are in abeyance, but my soul still works. Unerringly my knife follows the natural markings, slips into the natural cleavages, finds its way into the natural cavities. And so by conforming my work to the structure with which I am dealing, I have arrived at a point at which my knife never touches even the smallest ligament or tendon, let alone the main gristle.

A good carver changes his knife once a year; by which time the blade is dented. An ordinary carver changes it once a month; by which time it is broken. I have used my present knife for nineteen years, and during that time have carved several thousand bulls. But the blade still looks as though it has just come out of the mould.[19]

The words of Ting the Taoist butcher, told by the philosopher Chuang Tzu in the third century BC, are an extreme expression of the ideal of soft power. His actions as a butcher are "as carefully timed as the movements of a dancer in The Mulberry Wood"—he is an active decision maker. At the same time, he conforms his work to the structure with which he is dealing. He does not "wear himself out by useless conflict with the unchangeable laws of existence."[20] In other words, he goes with the flow, a master of line recognition. That doesn't mean necessarily that he's the ancient Chinese butcher we should be emulating. Maybe there was another guy who had a great deal more fun than Ting, despite having to purchase more knives. Seems possible.

On a two-wheeled vehicle, sometimes the flow of the trail is in the grooves, the "natural cleavages" where water would run; other times not. It may be more efficient, easier, to lift the tire onto or over a rock rather than trying to steer around it. Sometimes it may be easiest to simply let the tire impact a rock or root without trying to actively lift it, if the front of the obstacle is low enough, rounded or ramp-shaped. Mountain bike tires are made to bounce off of things, and it's a useful trait. Make the most of it, without overdoing it.

On the other hand, it may be preferable to steer around the obstacle completely. Or, it may be best to compromise and avoid it partially, by lifting the tire over an edge or just clipping it. Instead of turning with the tire on the dirt, it may be better or easier to simply pick up the front tire and move it over to one side or the other. A lot depends on speed, actual and desired. Maybe some of those ancient butchers who needed to buy knives more often than Ting carved twice as many bulls.

Turning too much, in a never-ending quest for the ultrasmooth line, might make for a very smooth ride but a very slow one, in terms of forward progress, and might ultimately cost more energy than a style that appears more crude and "violent." Rolling into and over things will not be nearly as smooth, but it could be a lot more direct. We can trade one type of exertion—lifting and manipulating the bike's front end—for another: controlling the machine as it bounces roughly into and over the obstacle. Trade-offs—again. To some extent, the rider gets to choose his or her own personal mix of turning, lifting, and banging. The most efficient choice will be determined by body type and riding style; bike type and suspension setup; level of fatigue and various individualized whims and preferences. Depending on the rider, the best choice may not be the most efficient. Or, there might not be a best choice. At some point, it turns philosophical.

Obviously, there are times when a trail doesn't offer more than one or two choices for a given skill-set—some objects you have to go over, and some you have no choice but to go around. Personally, when given a choice, I like to smooth out the trail with liberal twisting and turning of the wheels. (This has the bonus effect of making the ride longer.) Like lots of folks, however, I enjoy just bashing off rocks and roots and launching through the air—occasionally for no good reason, occasionally because launching right over something is sometimes a fine way to get past it. It's a matter of style. For the most part, I err on the side of smooth. The smoothest line may not be the fastest line, but it's always the smoothest.

Clearly, there are many possibilities when choosing a line and many choices to be made. If we and our bikes can roll over big rocks and roots, or twist around them, depending largely on what we prefer, that's important news. This opens up more of the trail for our use, makes more lines possible. More importantly, it means that "getting knocked off line" doesn't have to knock us off the bike. With a relaxed, adaptive style, we can get bounced or coerced from one line to another, maintain our balance, and just keep rolling. It's a good thing for us that riding with total control and perfect precision is unnecessary, because it's also impossible.

A TALE OF TWO LINES: REAR The

beginner phase of trail riding is spent figuring out how and where to steer the visible front tire, and the rear just trails along behind, out of sight and out of mind. The rear's ability to trail passively becomes a bit of a get-out-of-jail-free card for clumsy trail jockeys. As long as you can get that front wheel up and over an object, the rear will bang into and over it as well. At least, most of the time—until it creates some deal-breaking impact or loses traction and washes out.

That clunky style of riding was fine for the '80s and '90s, when everybody was a rookie. Eventually we learned to manage the rear tire along with the front, and it was good. It should come as no surprise that mountain biking becomes smoother, faster, easier, and more enjoyable when our rear wheel rolls around or glides over some of the objects it used to encounter violently and clumsily.

We tend to think of the mountain bike as a singular vehicle, but it is better and much more accurate to think of it as a pair of wheels with two distinct and separate lines.* The two wheels will enter any given section of trail at different times and likely at different locations.

The two lines are separate but not *independent*. The path of the rear tire, the follower, is a complicated function of the line chosen for the front tire. In a turn the rear tire will always track inside the front. In a steady-state turn (there is no such thing in real life), the tires would trace concentric circles; the tighter the turn, the greater the distance between the two circles, approaching a maximum distance equal to the wheelbase of the bike. If the front tire follows a sine curve, the rear will make a sinusoidal curve of lesser amplitude, phase-shifted behind the front. Things rapidly get more complicated from there. Given the much more complex real-life movements of a bicycle front tire, the rear line can only be *approximated* through the mathematical backdoor using a kind of differential calculus known as a Riccati equation.[21]

---

* Still more accurately, the bike can be conceptualized as two separate, moving "contact patches," the small areas where the tires actually meet dirt.

Experienced trail riders aren't out there calculating Riccati functions in their heads, but have nonetheless developed a very precise feel for the path of the rear tire based on the steering they impart to the front. This rear tire awareness is an important part of what it means to "become one with the machine." When the rider knows what the rear wheel is going to do a second or two before it does it, that's a powerful advantage which enables proactive management of body position and both lines.

Often it's the mere awareness of the rear line that enables a higher level of technical prowess. It doesn't take much. With basic, easy steering moves, an awakened rider begins to improve the rear tire's path. First of all, one learns that the bike steers a bit like a semitruck. The front end has to turn wider around an obstacle because the rear end will always track closer (as long as it stays on the ground). As a truck driver, if you don't make extra-wide turns, you start crunching newspaper boxes and hotdog stands with the rear end. It's not just about turns though. Any obstacle in the trail exposes the two-line reality. For instance, it often happens that the best way of dealing with a rock in the middle of the trail is by passing the front tire on one side and the back tire on the other. And yet somehow we still envision and speak of one line.

Expert riders learn to move the rear tire around by steering the front in a certain way. Occasionally it may be necessary to make a crazy-looking, exaggerated turn of the front wheel just to affect a small squiggle in the rear, to slip smoothly around a rock. At other times you may need to hold the front line straight longer than you otherwise would, long enough to usher the rear tire through the same slim gap through which the front just passed.

Even the best bike handlers are unlikely to learn how to manipulate the rear as well as they control the front. It is possible, however, to alter and manipulate the rear line in direct ways. One can free the rear tire of its front tire master, just for a moment, either by lifting it above the ground or sliding it along the dirt. To do this, shift body mass, apply brakes to either wheel, lift up on the pedals with the feet, twist the grips forward, or use some combination of these techniques. This kind of direct manipulation is useful for tight switchbacks, unweighting or lifting the back tire onto obstacles to reduce impact, and for finessing the rear end around rocks at

speed, with a little sideways slide. Loose riders can break traction deliberately and skid-slide the rear end out, maybe 6 inches or a foot, maybe just
an inch or two, depending on what is needed to snake around an obstacle
or to create a more comfortable angle for a turn. That's one of the sweetest
little moves on two wheels.

Special problems emerge for our dualistic machine when the distance between two obstacles ahead is roughly equal to the wheelbase of
the bicycle. In this situation the rear tire's contacting and rolling over
its obstacle might force the front tire downward at the moment it has to
be lifted up. A particularly savvy rider will see and sense which *pairs* of
obstacles will be problematic, and if possible will adjust lines to avoid
striking both objects at once.

Managing the rear wheel doesn't mean rolling scot-free around every
single chunk. As with the front, at some point all those tight little turns
and lifts of the wheel would be more trouble than they're worth. Some
degree of banging and bouncing is not only inevitable, but useful. Each
individual will have to determine how far he or she wants to take rear-
wheel management, and when it is best to just let the thing trail passively,
based on riding style, bike setup, and specific trail conditions. The primary point is to consider the rear line along with the front—don't just
forget about it. Smashing the rear wheel into an obstacle in a less-than-
elegant fashion should be the result of a conscious decision, and even if it
isn't, the rider should at least be able to forecast any unwanted impact and
adjust body position accordingly.

PROPELLING THE BIKE The front line is the
favored line, the steering line, and a major prime-time television show.
The front wheel deserves special care because its specific alignment is
critically important for the overall control of the bike (i.e., not wrecking).
The rear doesn't hold nearly as much significance for safety, but deserves
its own special consideration for another reason: The rear wheel is the
drive wheel.

So the bike is not as much like a semitruck as it seemed to be in the
last section. It is not right to say that the front is the tractor and the rear

is the trailer, as the backside of the bike is pushing the front. The force of pedaling must be coordinated with the movements of the front tire, to ensure that the two aren't working at cross-purposes. If the rider tries to mash the pedals while the front wheel is turned sharply into the side of the trail (an exceedingly common mistake), the bike's not going anywhere. At least give your bike a chance of doing what you want it to.

Straight-ahead traction under the drive tire should be among the factors weighing on the rider's decision of how and where to direct the bike along the trail. The rear tire doesn't necessarily have to be on something solid all the time, only at the moment when the rider *needs* to exert rotational force on it through the chain. Experts develop a sense for when they can apply full pedaling force and when they have to soft-pedal, based on the location of the rear contact patch over varied terrain.

In addition to these tuned-in soft-power strategies, which involve timing and smoothing the force of pedaling, some simple and relatively crude body movements can also help the bike accelerate more effectively. To increase traction on any surface, the grips can be twisted backward with each pedal stroke to force the rear tire down a little bit more, and body position can be shifted back—slide the rear end back on the saddle—for small and huge differences in traction, respectively.

Symptoms of traction failure are obvious. The tire spins in place, occasionally throwing back the babyhead chunk of rock upon which it had been allowed to meander. When the trail rider presses forward on the pedals, only to feel the rear tire give way suddenly—it can even knock the breath out a little—the bicyclist feels the pain of the marauding bandit in the north of China, striking furiously at a disappearing Tai Chi monk and left deflated and powerless. Don't blow your Chi by trying to push off against a platform that doesn't exist.

On sketchy surfaces, traction is intimately related to pedaling cadence. A cycling enthusiast might proclaim that one should always try to pedal at a fast cadence, over 100 revolutions per minute (rpm). Usually, this is something the enthusiast reads in a magazine article somewhere. Maybe this is part of a conspiracy to sell more bottom brackets. The truth is that optimum cadence is highly variable depending on terrain, highly variable among individual riders,* and highly variable depending on what you're trying to accomplish out there. (Are you racin' or ramblin'?)

More than any other bicycling discipline, cross-country trail riding is associated with high-cadence pedaling in the conventional wisdom. This association is largely illusory, as off-road climbing cadence is really pretty low in the grand scheme. In reality, track racers and road racers both turn more rpm than mountain bikers; BMX racers and competitors in other start-gate disciplines all turn the pedals much faster out of the gate and turns. Mountain bikers use the lowest gears, but not the fastest cadence. On the trail, rpm *seem* very high because the gears are relatively tiny and there are a lot of pedal revolutions *compared to the speed of travel*. On the road, a 100-rpm cadence at 25 mph seems about right, works well. A 100-rpm cadence at 5 mph on a steep climb—maybe too much pedaling. The same cadence will seem much faster on the trail, at low speed.

Novice trail riders seem to err on the high-rpm side, which is probably for the best when it's all said and done. They learn to climb steep hills in the granny gear—it's the only way it can be done at first. Then, as their bodily systems adapt and all the associated skills sharpen, they're often still attached to that tiny gear even though it's not suitable anymore. They simply spin faster and faster to compensate. It's hard to let go of that precious granny, like Linus with his blanket. To a degree, that's fine. It's useful to develop a good spinning technique. Working low gears will preserve energy on long rides, and it's difficult to hurt oneself by riding too low gears. However, spinning too fast will be more trouble than it's worth and will also hinder one's ability to get over rocky or rooty sections. *Counterproductive* is a good word for it.

---

* "I have often been told that I use gears that are too big in the mountains. I don't think this is true. I always choose my gears according to the pedaling cadence that suits me. Above this cadence I get out of breath too quickly. Below it, my muscles are too contracted and the blood doesn't flow through them. For me, a good climbing rhythm is somewhere between 70 and 90 revolutions per minute," writes five-time Tour de France winner Bernard Hinault, referring to his road technique.[22] Former Tour de France contender Levi Leipheimer notes some the cadence differences involved in off-road cycling: "In general, a slower cadence in a higher gear will offer more stability when negotiated [sic] rough, technical terrain. Having that extra resistance will make it much easier to go up, over, and/or around obstacles without losing momentum. Let's say you're on very rutted terrain. You want a real big gear and slow cadence to put your weight on your feet, easing the pain on your butt. (The harder of a gear you're pushing, the less your butt rests on the saddle.) . . . What it boils down [to] is that, in most cases, you'll have a better experience if you push a bigger gear on your mountain bike instead of spinning at 90rpm."[23]

On technical climbs, fast cadence causes problems in a few ways. The main bugaboo is excessive up-down motion of the butt, upper body, and head caused by furious egg-beater pedaling—almost any up-down motion, really, can be considered excessive. That's wasted motion, wasted energy, not to mention ugly, bad mountain biking. Bouncy pedaling will also undermine traction when you need it most, as it rhythmically unweights the back tire. Putting a very low gear on a loose surface is also inappropriate, bouncing or not. As with driving on slippery roads, shifting up a bit will help the rear tire hook up on a loose trail.

So the excessive spinner is bouncing up and down, not really moving forward, spitting rocks and gravel out the back for a moment, then clipping out. If that describes you, try the same hill in a bigger gear and see if that alone doesn't smooth everything out. Using a bigger gear doesn't necessarily mean applying more force to the pedals, just different force. Road-racing super-legend Bernard Hinault, a student of the arcane details of pedaling technique, notes the smoothing effect of big gears: "Since your legs are rotating slower, it's easier to change the direction of force, trying to keep it perpendicular to the crank arm." [24]

While using larger gears can have immediate positive effects over rough ground, it is extremely important not to overdo the gear inches, as this causes a dangerous sort of strain on the joints and the various cords and connective tissues, especially around the knee. At the first sign of knee pain, or lower back pain that seems to be caused by pedaling strain, shift to a lower gear and slow down. Don't think to yourself, *I'll just work through this,* a simple thought with potentially disastrous long-term consequences. Instead of jumping right into bigger gears, sneak up on them a little bit, a gear at a time. Give your body plenty of time to adapt, perhaps years. It's pretty common for very fit and experienced riders to reach a level where they reserve the little chainring for rare occasions, but it takes a while to get there. Improvements in technical skill are almost as important as improvements in muscular strength for enabling the use of larger gears.

Given that cadence is individualized, find the rhythm that suits you best at your current level of fitness and skill. Just make sure you're somewhere between that counterproductive hyperspin and the injurious over-gear at all times, and work on developing your own style based on your own specific attributes and talents. Just like different types of bikes and equipment, different gears have different pros and cons. It's wise to try to get comfortable with a wide range of gears and cadences. On singletrack, there isn't necessarily one right gear for a particular situation. Whatever gear you're onto, work it with some finesse.

It's easy to see the theme of this section: Pedal smooth circles. On technical sections, however, don't forget that the bike is equipped with a ratcheting mechanism called a freewheel. Backpedal briefly (typically one half-pedal rev) to adjust the timing of the crankarm's downstroke, as needed to keep the pedal from striking a rock or root. Experts tap this important technique at least a few times per ride, occasionally a few times through a single rock garden.

OUT OF THE SADDLE John Howard, the American road racer who dominated the domestic racing scene in the ten or fifteen years prior to Greg Lemond, and who is perhaps best known for powering a bicycle across the Bonneville Salt Flats at 152 mph, came up with a rule about climbing hills on a mountain bike. "The rule," he writes, "is that you should never leave the saddle unless it is absolutely necessary."[25] Howard was a big man with femurs longer than table legs who could always generate an overabundance of power while seated, and we should expect him to hold some different ideas about the ideal climbing position than the rest of us. With all due respect to Howard, a living legend, a force of nature, his statement is false. There is no such rule.

"If anything," says Travis R., a Colorado veteran, "People stay seated way too much while climbing. . . . They should get off their butts more often for a more dynamic position."

Another trailhound disagrees, but he's on different equipment. "I like to stay seated basically all the time on climbs. With my 'full-sus' [full suspension] doing the dirty work, I can sit down and power without worrying too much about smoothing out the bumps. With that bike it seems silly to stand up like I would on my other bike." He's got extra bikes, and extra riding styles.

I rode behind one guy for a while and saw he was standing a lot, so I asked him about it. "I climb that way whenever conditions allow," he said. "It just suits my style better." Turns out he had spent the past several years exclusively on a single speed, working relatively huge gears on the climbs. On the SS he often needed the leverage of standing to keep rolling; eventually, he learned all kinds of tricks to maintain momentum on climbs at low rpm, as single-speeders do, and adapted his style to a geared bike. He was fast.

There are as many rules for out-of-saddle climbing as there are mountain bikers. In fact, there are many more rules than that, as each rider has different rules for different bikes and different days, as well as for different phases within the same ride. Experiment with all the versions of seated pedaling and non-seated pedaling to find out what suits your personal style and local terrain.

Relax when standing on the pedals, and let the bike rock back and forth while the upper body stays *relatively* still. Feel the leverage as your own weight falls onto the pedal as it comes over the top of the stroke. It may be possible to "dig" for additional traction by working the back tire over more so that its side-most knobs are pushed into the ground as the pedals come down.

Stand straight and tall on the pedals not only to add leverage, but also to rest and stretch the muscles on long, steady climbs; this causes a piston-like one-two stroke. Crouch lower, closer to the bike, with limbs very bent, in order to power the cranks in smooth circles at higher rpm—good for more aggressive acceleration and pedaling across rough ground. "Just get a full suspension. It's the same thing," says one guy. I don't completely agree, but I see his point.

Out-of-saddle climbing on a suspension fork can be problematic if it causes excessive energy loss through useless vertical motion. Locking out the shock turns it into a solid but dead set of pillars. This stops up-down movement but gives a less-than-optimal feel. A good, light rigid fork functions as a very tight spring, and feels correspondingly lively. Trade-offs.

Since traction is usually a little bit more troublesome while standing, specialists in out-of-saddle climbing keep their senses alert for patches of exceptional traction that will enable the technique. Slickrock, granite, and other types of rock outcroppings make especially conducive surfaces. Traction is so good on some rock faces, riders can lean out over the front of the bike and climb a steeper slope than would be possible on dirt. Similarly, on days after rain, the entire trail might be so perfectly tacky that riders can climb out of the saddle at will—also weave erratically, turn pirouettes, do whatever they want without breaking traction. Dave Wiens, the local endurance hero, likens such conditions to "powder days" on skis: "On the mountain bike, this is synonymous to trails with just the right amount of moisture in them to make them hard and tacky. Your bike carves like a pair of shape skis and the surface rolls fast."[26]

Most days aren't like that.

CORNERING AND BRAKING If you have

to think about *how* to corner while you're doing it, you're most likely doing it wrong. Cornering on a mountain bike works just like cornering on any other bike, except the surface is bumpy, rocky, off-camber, sandy, loose, muddy, radioactive, and on fire. Otherwise, it's exactly the same.

Turning a bike at speed is impossibly simple and impossibly complicated all at once. The bike is turned when it is leaned over. Steering the handlebars doesn't turn the bike, but it helps control the lean. If you start thinking about it, you're cooked. It has to be unconscious.* If it's not, try going to an abandoned parking lot or other large tarmac surface and swoop around—get the feel of laying the bike over to make it turn, until it feels natural. Then do the same on some flat, clean dirt and feel the added sensation of the tires slipping on the surface as the g-forces increase. Try some really sharp, deep turns. Check the limits of what the bike-rider system can do. You won't have to turn nearly so sharply on the singletrack, most likely, but this will train your body for the basic movements involved in turning a bike.

---

* Gallwey wondered about "unconscious" action in *The Inner Game of Tennis:* "How can you be consciously unconscious? It sounds like a contradiction in terms; yet this state can be achieved. Perhaps a better way to describe the player who is 'unconscious' is by saying that his mind is so concentrated, so focused, that it is still. It becomes one with what the body is doing, and the unconscious or automatic functions are working without interference from thoughts. The concentrated mind has no room for thinking how well the body is doing, much less of the how-to's of the doing."[27]

On the dirt, diving into fast curves will cause both tires to slide. That's a good thing! That's a lot of what mountain biking is all about in my local zone, where many of the trails are smooth, dry, and slippery. Ideally, riders get very comfortable with this two-wheel drift, or even relish it. Sometimes they even go out of their way to create it, a sort of hard-power preemptive strike on the gravel, by pushing their bikes into the turns in a slightly exaggerated fashion. It's very useful to get inside the slide, so to speak, understand it. Instead of worrying about avoiding or stopping tire drift, start to work it. By initiating the drift, a rider begins to learn exactly how the tires and dirt will interact on that day, gets a feel for the transitions and limits of traction. When the bike starts to slide, the rider must be very relaxed, supple, over the machine to maintain balance.

Instead of thinking about how to turn, simply look ahead at the trail surface, gather the information there, and turn. Of particular importance is the concavity of the trail. A lot of trails are noticeably concave, sloping upward at the edges. Some are veritable half-pipes. Use the banking to turn at much higher speed than would otherwise be possible—just like NASCAR and bicycle track racing. Man-made or groomed trails often feature really large, steep berms to enable really grandiose turns. Good times. Even a miniscule, 2-inch rise at the edge of the trail might be used to support the bike in a turn, if the lip is compacted enough.

The opposite of a nice bermed turn is an off-camber one. Instead of a banked turn, it's a negative banking. There's no magic cure for it; the maximum speed around a negative-banked turn must be lower, due to the laws of physics. For all curves, but especially those of the off-camber persuasion, always look through the turn to its exit, and beyond, or you may not make it that far.

While cornering, experiment with leaning the bike and body at different angles—different from each other. Don't hold the bike and body in one long line, except for rare occasions. Tweak it and bend it this way and that, and feel how doing so works the tires into the dirt in different ways. Try cornering with the feet in different positions. Notice how stomping the outside foot down solidly at the six o'clock position forces the tires to grab.

Braking, in my opinion, is another something you shouldn't be thinking about while the ride is in progress. As long as the equipment is reasonably well maintained, what is there to think about? Rightfully, not much. If you want to slow down, squeeze the lever. A little or a lot, depending. When the brakes are applied, the body weight tries to move to the front of the bike. This is true with either the front or rear brake. Practice intense braking moves to understand the kind of body finesse that is used to neutralize that force. More than you think, probably, if you're thinking about it. The harder the braking, the more amplified the body movement. Like a turn, it should all happen almost unconsciously. The timing is such that it must happen automatically, or it won't happen right. As with cornering, it is possible to train the body to respond automatically to braking forces with simple drills that can be practiced on pavement.

While riding at speed, say descending quickly on moderately technical ground, the body is over the bike in a relaxed, suspended position, and a finger or two or three, depending on personal preference, is/are "covering" the brake levers—not squeezing them but ready to. Riders who are in the habit of squeezing too much can descend while "fisting" one or both grips (holding it with no finger on the lever). Try using only the front brake for a while, then only the back. You'll see that both ways are possible, and very different. This will give you an appreciation for using both brakes at the same time, which is almost always the best method.

One often hears "You've got to have good brakes to go fast," or something cute like that. That might make sense for motor sports—where competitors accelerate toward a turn until the last possible instant, slam on the brakes as much as they can without spinning out, then summon upwards of 1,000 horsepower upon exit—but it doesn't translate very well to cross-country, with its distinct lack of massive internal-combustion engines. We are much more interested in conserving momentum.

Descending fast on a bike isn't about brakes. In mountain biking, if you want to go fast, lay *off* the brakes. If you want to slow down, on the other hand, them brakes are mighty fine. In fact, a good trail rider does not need powerful brakes to stylishly rage upon a singletrack trail; even with a lot of gnarly downhill, he or she just needs brakes that function reasonably well.

The stopping power of mountain bike brakes has improved hugely over the decades, as we have gone from cantilevers to V-brakes to discs. However, for most forms of American trail riding, we had plenty of stopping power with Dia Compe 987s. After all, if it can skid your tire, why do you need more power than that—to skid harder? Makes no sense. Disc brakes are a clear improvement in many ways over the old rim brakes, but their presence on cross-country bikes has given some people a warped idea about the necessities of extreme braking power for normal trail riding. Admittedly, it is quite nice to summon a good deal of braking with a small flick of one finger. The older brakes required a bit more hand jive. Some bike people say that disc brakes should be applied at full power and released, that they should be on or off and not in between; I think riders should try to get as much modulation as they can out of the mechanism. Lightly feathering the brakes is a useful method of control.

Too much focus on braking is a product of poor trail vision, and an element of the Cycle of Failure. The rider fights him- or herself, hyper-tenses the forearms and hands, receives a head-to-toe rattling from the bumps, and, critically, looks hard at the area just in front of the bike. Looking farther down the trail may be all that's needed to free the mind, and free the grip from the levers. Consciously relax the arms and upper body. Also, try some of that deep breathing. In any case, it's not about braking performance.

Concerning traction, think of it as a single pizza pie that can be divided between cornering and braking. Maybe cornering wants one piece, which leaves seven pieces for braking. Maybe each wants half the pie. If braking eats the whole pie, there won't be any left over. The trail rider can hit the brakes hard, or hit the turn hard. Trying to hit both hard at the same time might be difficult, or impossible, depending on the surface. A rider who is comfortable in the slide and understands the surface can utilize aggressive cornering and braking that would make a tense rider slide out and crash.

The front brake is more effective than the rear brake. In a hard stop on the road, the front brake does almost all the work—the rear is off the ground, or kind of skittering along the pavement, unable to donate much stopping power to the overall effort. On the dirt, rear brakes seem to be much more important and useful. It's a lot easier to skid the front tire on dirt, which means braking has to be somewhat more dainty. Still, the front brake can impart more g-force deceleration on the dirt as well.

In hard-braking situations, during which the bike is often tilted downward to begin with and therefore more likely to pitch forward, the rear end can come off the ground rather easily. While descending rocky trails with moderate steps and drops, even light braking can levitate the back end. New rider panics and goes over for a tumble; the experienced rider adjusts body position seamlessly and controls the bike, momentarily riding the front wheel down the mountain. It's not like that's the desired configuration for a descent, but it doesn't have to cause a crash. With experience one learns that there is a great deal of leeway between the point when the rear tire levitates, and the point of no return when the bike goes over.

When your tires start to wear out, you'll notice that braking performance disintegrates along with them. With knobs critically diminished, the tires under heavy deceleration break traction much sooner than normal, slipping suddenly, surprisingly, and significantly. Time for new tires, or a new way of riding.

A NATURAL HISTORY OF DIRT The

Rocky Mountains seem to owe their existence to their location on the North American tectonic plate. As the plate smashed around the globe, banging into and pulling away from other plates, helping to form the mysterious proto-continents Columbia, Rodinia, Pannotia, Pangaea, and several others, over many hundreds of millions of years, it broke apart in the area where it is most thin, and the pieces were shoved upward. Lucky.

Actually, those pieces seem to have been shoved upward several times, according to geologists, and after each period of upward-shoving the forces of erosion diminished the peaks severely, while their slopes were covered in layers of sediment. The most recent period of mountain-building occurred about fifty million years ago. Now we are here watching the granite mountains again being steadily beaten down by erosion. But not just watching. We are lucky enough to help, just a little, in the process of eroding them again.

The rock that forms Pikes Peak, and, in its massiveness, a nice chunk of the Front Range of the Colorado Rockies, was created deep in the earth from slowly cooling magma about a *billion* years ago. You know, give or take a few hundred million. Pikes Peak granite is a bona fide geologic time traveler at our feet, having been around for everything from theoretical proto-continents to Lady Gaga. It's been here through the rise and fall of several different global ecosystems, and it will see the rise and fall of many more. The Appalachians were shoved upward at the edge of the North American plate and began their latest erosional process several hundred million years *earlier* than Pikes Peak and the Rockies. Still, the old Appalachians have only been around for about 10 percent of the earth's estimated lifespan.

To better understand the scale of geologic time, stand and spread your arms out to your sides, as far as they'll go. Let your awesome wingspan, from fingertip to fingertip, represents the age of the earth. Now take a fingernail file and give your most distant fingernail a quick one-two. You have just removed from the tip of your fingernail the portion of geologic time that represents the entire history of humankind.[28]

See, we are nothing but a nasty little rash on the earth. A flare-up.

Anyway, as long as you've digested the fact of your unbelievably brief, speck-like existence, which makes even the smallest soil particle laugh, you will be in the proper state of mind to appreciate the dirt beneath your tires.

Dirt is important. The dirt of the earth forms a relatively tiny skin around the planet, yet sustains all plant life and, by extension, all animal life, including you. Everything springs from the dirt in some sense.* So, we come from the dirt, and we'll go back to it. But where did the dirt come from?

---

* Soil supports plant growth in critical ways, but the vast majority of actual plant material is created from the carbon dioxide in the air through photosynthesis. When a tree decays, the CO_2 goes back into the atmosphere, part of the earth's carbon balance. This balance has gone haywire, due to the nasty rash known as humans and their insistence on extracting massive amounts of concentrated carbon from deep in the earth and blowing it into the atmosphere in a hundred-year orgy of combustion. Mountain bikers, unfortunately, tend to be some of the most intense carbon-spewers to come around in the past 4.5 billion years. Mountain biking may be a soft art, but it's also an automobile-intensive one, overall.

One of the first steps in the erosional process can be seen easily from the road up Pikes Peak: the weathering of granite and its gradual conversion to soil. Mica crystals in the granite slowly decompose, especially when exposed to moisture, changing into clay minerals. But the clay minerals take up more space than the previous micas, swelling and loosening the quartz crystals that form much of the body of the rock. The swelling process is augmented by frost crystals and, on cold nights, turns to ice. The process gradually weakens the granite, forming a deep layer of soft "rotten" granite, the first step in the making of soil.[29]

Mountains make soil. The pre-everything rock washed down from above becomes the base material, but it is just one of four necessary components needed for the creation of actual, plant-bearing soil. The pedosphere, as the realm of soil is known, is defined as the intersection of all the other 'spheres: stratosphere, hydrosphere, lithosphere, and biosphere. Air, water, minerals, living and dead organic material, right there at our feet, mixing it up. Without any one of those elements, it's no longer soil, although it may still be dirt.

The trail isn't soil. Unless it's brand-new, the soilness has been beaten out of it, ground down to nothing and blown away. The lack of these soil ingredients is sort of what defines the trail in relation to its immediate surroundings. Soil is created by the addition of air, water, and biotic material to weathered rock. The trail is created through the opposite process—the removal of the less durable components in soil.

For mountain biking purposes, the most important characteristic of the dirt is probably its simple structure, or *fabric*—the way it's put together. This includes the shape and size of the soil solids (including minerals and organic substances) and the amount of air between them. Trail riders might take note of the fabric of the trail, first of all, in terms of four basic particle sizes: gravel, sand, silt, and clay. (Pedologists don't worry too much about gravel, as anything larger than sand is getting pretty non-soil-like.) These particles will be arranged in wildly different proportions on different trails, and the arrangement largely determines how the trail wears and how it rides.

The trails of the Pikes Peak area are made of particles that are comparatively huge—a gravel aggregate called *grus*. There are lots of completely unformed, gravelly sections, especially on steep climbs. Riding the *grus* can be kind of like jumping into all those plastic balls in the inflatable castle. This makes drive traction extremely tricky, and turns are slippery as well. Lots of riders who aren't used to it express an extreme dislike for the sketchy *grus,* which is found above Colorado Springs and throughout an area stretching about 50 miles to the northwest. On the other hand, the gravel has some upside. The trails are often smooth and fast for significant distances, with only sporadic rock problems. Often the gravel itself is the most challenging technical feature. And the drainage characteristics are outstanding. During or after rain, the *grus* is glued together somewhat by moisture, creating excellent traction, and puddles are few. The water runs right through it.

Trails of generally similar performance exist throughout the West, but are hardly the rule. Most of the mountains aren't quite so brittle, and so provide a different sort of parent material. A lot of the trails in the region are composed of smaller particles, more dark organic matter, and more frequent rock features. Such a surface may allow for more aggressive turning and braking—braking later and harder, leaning the bike over more at higher speeds—but this advantage is often negated by the additional rocks.

On the other end of the spectrum from the *grus* are trails composed primarily of tiny particles. Clay-dominant surfaces can be rock-hard when completely dry, depending on the climate where they're located. When the clay is wet, it becomes very difficult to deal with. Serious mud. Notice how tire tracks or footprints slopped into the clay when wet are preserved in its concrete-like surface when dry, creating little complications/opportunities. Clay trails are often fast, but unforgiving. The Telegraph Trail near Durango is a good example of a clay singletrack in a semiarid climate.

Climbing upward from Durango, or Colorado Springs, or any number of places that sit at the foot of mountains, the landscape changes without subtlety. Different trees appear—fir and spruce and aspen instead of the rugged ponderosa pine and Gambel oak. A bit more water falls from the sky. The ground is covered with a green layer instead of yellow grasses and cactus. Elk instead of mule deer. Shade. And consequently there are very different soil properties evident as elevation is gained. In the pine forests, the soil and the trails contain more decomposing organic material: aspen leaves, pine needles, pine cones, twigs, elk droppings, the carcasses of a vast menagerie of microscopic creatures. Dirt is different in the mountains.

Out east, we tend to find more moisture and plant material in the trail fabric. Rolling from a dry Pikes Peak–style surface to a Pisgah-style surface would be a fairly drastic change, with big differences in rolling resistance and traction. Even the sound of the tires on the dirt would change noticeably. Trails in the eastern United States tend to be darker, muddier, tighter. The landscape is much leafier, with lots of shrubbery closing in on the singletrack. (Trails in the Northwest and Southeast are even darker, muddier, leafier.) Naturally the root factor is relatively high as well. More trees, more roots. Many northeastern trail systems, like "Vietnam" in Massachusetts, are notoriously rocky and technical. Not everything out east fits that bill, however. The Tsali trails, for instance, are about as smooth and flowy as the trails around Pikes Peak (with less gravel).

It's unwise to generalize about the trails in any given area of the country. No matter what region you're in, you'll likely find wide variation in trail characteristics within it. Most singletrack trails in the United States provide some mix of smooth flow and technical sections. Some riders prefer smooth speed; others prefer more technical challenges. Most of us like to find some of both during a trail ride.

Which part of the nation has the *best* trails? Easy—whichever part you're in right now.

TIRES: THE INTERFACE
Tires are your ambassadors to the different worlds of dirt. Probably more than any other equipment choice, tires affect the feel of the machine. And still, there is no surefire right or wrong here, just a wide range of personal preferences, based on subjective impressions and superstitions.

There are several types of tread from which to choose, depending on what kind of dirt you ride, and how you like to ride it. Generally speaking, a tire with big, widely spaced "knobs" will be better for loose conditions and for grabbing rock edges, and a tire with shorter, firmer knobs will work better for hardpack. (Another way of putting that: Tires with big, widely spaced knobs *only* work well in very loose conditions, like the local bog.) On softer surfaces—softer than the tire—the tire's knobs will dig into the dirt. In some small but significant way, the tire is actually altering the trail. On the hard stuff, however, the knobs will behave badly, twisting around awkwardly while providing no extra traction. Riders of off-road motorcycles know that their lumpy off-road tires can cause serious control issues on pavement. Same concept here.

Front and rear tires have different demands for traction, and thus may very well have different tread patterns. Front tires don't need to worry about propelling the bike forward, so the knobs are better arranged for rolling speed and cornering bite. The rear tire's tread is often arranged more like a paddle wheel, for obvious reasons. Some tread patterns work fine on either end.

Off-road tire technology is one of the many areas where marketing has kind of taken over from science. It can be difficult to identify genuine breakthroughs among the advertising hype. What seems a breakthrough to one rider will be, to another equally experienced individual, completely wrong. "In the late '80s," according to the late, great Sheldon Brown, "there was a revolution in tread design, started by the Specialized Ground Control. This tire, and many later MTB tires, had tall knobs at the side of the tread, with extra bracing to keep the knobs from being bent away from the centerline of the tire. These knobs greatly improved performance in sand and mud, because as a section of the tire rolls into contact with the ground, it flattens out. This flattening out causes the outer knobs to bend inward, so that they grab a loose surface like a pair of pliers."[30] Pliers, eh? Whether or not that's a good thing is up for debate. Wouldn't that also slow you down sometimes?

Maxxis offers "EXO Technology"—"An extremely cut-resistant and abrasion-resistant material added to the sidewalls of select mountain tires. This densely woven material is also lightweight and highly flexible, ensuring that the performance of the tire remains unaffected."[31] If the material is so lightweight and flexible that it doesn't affect the performance of the tire, how much protection could it really add? Mountain bike tires shouldn't require extra sidewall protection anyway. I've always been leery of that particular scheme. The sidewall should be durable to begin with. In any case, hold onto your wallets when the tire salesmen come to town.

For cross-country riding, most riders who are aware of the difference prefer a relatively lightweight tire, with a high thread count (measured in threads per inch, or TPI) and a softer rubber compound. This translates into lower rolling resistance due to the suppleness of the tire casing, but more grip on the surface, like the bottom of a climbing shoe. These soft, light tires are also expensive and—bonus—wear out quite fast. Using them on pavement will cause the tread to wear quickly and visibly off-center, due to the slight slope engineered into the typical street for drainage purposes. This is just part of the punishment that should be meted out to those who abuse off-road tires on tarmac.

In addition to its tread pattern, a tire's width and volume will also affect the bike's attitude significantly. Big tires provide more suspension and roll nicely, but necessarily weigh a little more. Changes in air pressure will also cause drastic changes in handling characteristics. In fact, if your bike feels a little funky, or a lot funky, the first thing you should check is the air pressure.

Lots of folks are running tubeless setups these days, which, among other benefits, allows them to use lower air pressure without worrying about pinch-flats. Lower pressure has some nice effects, adding traction and smoothing out the bumps. What's the trade-off? It limits the max g-force of your turns. The tire's cross section has to remain basically round in the turn for the system to function. Very hardpacked, off-camber trails demand special attention in this regard. Off-camber, bermed—it doesn't really matter. Too hard of a turn on too soft a tire, and the tire might change shape just a little too much, sort of flop over onto one side of the rim, twist the wheel violently, and dump the rider even more violently. This kind of wreck happens occasionally as a result of undetected slow leaks.

Riding on very low pressure has become somewhat of a fad. Weird equipment fads come and go constantly in this sport. (Says a former user of Scott AT-4 handlebars. Google 'em.) If I were a betting man, I'd wager that the low-pressure fad will pass like a bad flu within about five years of this book's publication, and folks will be back to riding on round tires. We'll see.

It would be nice to have a different set of tires for every possible condition—different treads and widths, rubber compounds, colors to match your varied moods. But have you seen the price of tires these days? It's getting nuts out there. Unless you're a very obsessive racer, or a professional one, it's probably best to use one moderately treaded tire that will work on varied surfaces, based on your personal preferences and prejudices. Work with it until it wears out. Sometimes the tread pattern will be a great match, sometimes not so great. After all, surfaces change from foot to foot, not just from state to state. So having extra tires won't do you much good anyway, unless you bring them all along for the ride. You could strap them around your torso like bandoliers, and stop to change them out every few minutes.

After finding a style of tire that works very well for you on the trails you ride most, it may be worthwhile to keep using the same model for a long while, to become intimately acquainted with all sides of its distinctive personality.

STEP UP So you're climbing upward, upward. The trail is steep. Plenty steep. Your velocity? Slow crawl. Not too much gas left in the tank, so to speak. This is what you signed up for, a major workout. At the same time, if this trail doesn't tip over soon, there's going to be carnage. And then, around the next bend . . . Looks like some helpful Boy Scouts have been around to install a set of *steps* right there in the singletrack, using railroad ties or beams or something. Not cool, Boy Scouts.

If you were walking, traveling in the inherently clunky mode of the upright primate, these steps would be a welcome sight—steps provide the most efficient way for a human on foot to gain altitude in a hurry.[32] For a wheeled vehicle, ramps are what you want, obviously. A single step can stop you dead in your tracks, or even send you back down the mountain in tumbleweed mode. Steps are the jealous hiker's revenge.

Steplike features are some of the most consistently unwelcome, harassing features of singletrack trails. When a step-up is encountered during a steep climb—as it often is, due to the very nature of the thing—"cleaning" the obstacle will require an unholy combination of technical finesse (yin) and explosive power (yang). In some sense the trick of mountain biking boils down to this. A lot of the vexing technical features encountered on steep climbs are less extreme versions of this same problem. This means that riders who can handle the nastier types of step-ups can handle just about anything that the trail puts in their way. Rock climbers speak of the "crux" of a climb—the most difficult moment on a route, that point where all the climber's strength and skill needs to be concentrated. Get past the crux and the route is essentially conquered. Steplike features very often create a similar type of crux situation for bicyclists on an uphill section of singletrack.

Of course, most of the steps you'll encounter on the trail aren't man-made or Boy Scout–made, at least not directly. There are a few different types of natural steps found on singletrack trails, and riding up and over them requires different methods. Quite often it's just a big rock blocking the trail or a number of smaller rocks that form a single monolith. Another type of step is formed when a thick tree root crosses an inclined trail—or, more accurately, when a trail crosses a thick tree root. The root holds back the soil on the high side while the material below is washed away, leaving a deep trough and a steplike feature.

A rock is more likely than a root to provide ample traction for the rear tire. Some types of rock features are positively sticky. If traction is beckoning so loudly, the rider simply throws the front tire onto the top of the ledge, wheelie-ing the bike onto the formation. With the front tire on top and the rear tire crunched into the rock, the rider can use a crudely applied pedal stroke, or some combination of pedaling and finesse to continue up and over. There are several ways to deal with a step like that.

For a tall root-formed or rock step-up on an incline, with nothing substantial for a rear tire to grab and push against, there's really only one way to go about conquering the obstacle. It's hard. Without traction when we could use it most, only momentum and precision can get us over. The momentum is derived from power applied *before* the obstacle is reached, and it might have to be some pretty serious power. That's often a tall order when you're already beat from climbing the hill. The precision in the maneuver is derived from planning and visualization.

Look at how most attempts to ride a big step end: with the rider half-way up the obstacle, front tire on top and rear tire below, and one foot down on the dirt. Maybe cursing. *Halfwaysville.* This shows us that getting the front tire up is fairly easy, while getting the whole bike over is another matter entirely. The halfway-up rider is a symptom of the failure to visualize and plan for the entire multipart sequence of actions required to clean such an obstacle.

The first task when encountering a big root-formed step is to *look* for a good line. Don't think about finding the right line, or worry about the wrong line, just find one that you know you can ride. Decide where you want to put your tires, looking not only at the obstacle itself but also at the approach and the run-out—*look, decide, ride!* There it is, by golly, there it is. There may not be a slew of easy and obvious lines to find. Sometimes the trail may dictate only a few possibilities. And sometimes all you can decide is that there is *no* rideable line that matches your skill level or will level at that time, in which case the best course of action would be to roll gently to the obstacle and clip out, do the dirty work on foot, then remount. If you can't see a good line—if you can't imagine how you personally can get up the step with a bike attached to your feet—then you won't ride up the step, other than by some fluky accident.

The best line might be right up the middle; more likely it will be off to the side, where there tends to be less distance from trail surface to the top of the step. (Needless to say, don't go off-trail to poach a line more suitable to your limited skills.) Since it's on a hill and demands a lot of power, turning while attacking the obstacle is more difficult; thus it can also be difficult to create much distance between the front and rear lines on purpose. Even so, there is likely to be some distance between them, even if the rider tries to keep the bike as straight as possible, and any separation could be significant. Take care to usher the rear tire past any of the seemingly minor knots or chunks of rocks that are near the front tire's line. The difference between flowing onward and stepping out could come down to a tiny jag that blocks one knob on the back tire.

If the front tire is lifted through the air onto the step, without impact, problematic angles of attack only concern the rear line. The angle of the rear tire's encounter with the ledge/step/root can be changed drastically to suit the rider's desires by moving the front wheel laterally at the same time it is lifted onto the top of the obstacle. At relatively low forward speed, a big lateral move of the front tire causes the rear to pivot almost in place. If you have to lift the front tire anyway, make the most of it by fixing the rear line in the process.

After identifying the most inviting pair of lines, the rider must antici-pate and visualize just how much initial speed will be needed to carry the entirety of him- or herself and vehicle (not just the front half) up and over the crux on that path. It takes experience to know, or feel, how much speed will be required to win this battle with gravity and friction. Gener-ally at this point the rider will have to speed up from the normal climbing speed, sometimes a lot. Remember that the root provides little or no trac-tion for the rear tire, so once the front tire is lifted onto the step, there will be a moment without the opportunity to propel the bike using the drive-train. Carrying enough speed into the move is critical. (If the mountain biker is too tuckered to make the necessary speed, the root has already won. No use attempting the obstacle at that point.)

So you've found a line, can feel in your bones what kind of speed will be needed, and the engine room is responding by turning up the power. The power is applied smoothly on the dirt, no spinning out or bouncing, and translates nicely into increased speed. Just before the bike bangs into the root, use a pedal stroke to lift the front wheel onto the top of the ledge at the predetermined spot. Ideally this placement of the front tire is silent and seamless, right on top of the lip. It's better to err on the high side, lift it too far; too low and it impacts solidly, killing momentum or knocking you off. The tire is shaped for it, but this really isn't a good place for any sort of impact. This is another fading art—there's always room for improvement with front tire precision. Baseball is a game of inches; mountain biking a game of millimeters. Anyway, that's the easy part. This is the point where most riders panic and clip out, because they didn't think things through all the way, and didn't carry enough momentum to bring the rest of the bike onto the ledge.

A split second after the front tire is placed on the ledge, the rear will contact the root. So the rider, immediately after placing the front tire, must heave all his or her weight up and forward in an exaggerated motion, necessarily out of saddle. This *unweights* the rear of the bike just in time to allow it to follow the front tire onto the top of the step. The body move-ment here may be difficult for novices to visualize. It is substantial, quick, fluid, and total, from one end of the bike to the other—using the body mass to dominate and move the bike-rider system. Done ultrasmoothly, the rear tire makes only a kissing contact with the root. Realistically, there is likely to be some more substantial impact.

To ride up onto a tall step and past it, the mountain biker has employed virtually all the basic tools of trail riding: vision and visualization, planning and momentum, relaxation and spirited manipulation of body mass. To ride down the same steps, the same basic techniques are used, except no force needs to be applied to the pedals. With gravity on your side, get off the saddle on bent limbs and look for the line as it trails out away from the obstacle. As with the step-up, the step-down requires the rider to think the move through all the way, which in this case means finding a nice run-out to go with the technical route over the step. Don't seize on the obstacle itself—if your vision stops there, so will the bike.

RESTARTING ON A STEEP HILL

Should we even try?

When a rider fails to complete a steep climb and has to clip out, he or she is left with a dilemma. Trying to restart is likely to be tricky. Without any momentum at all, momentum zero, the rider must be ultrasmooth to accelerate what?—150 to 200 pounds, most likely, with bike and rider— from dead-zero mph on a steep hill, on the dirt. The weight, like weight everywhere, wants badly to fall backward off the bike and tumble down to the bottom of the hill where it belongs. This weight has to be perched just right over the bike and held there without struggle, and the force on the pedal must be so gently applied, the upper body so calm and relaxed, to make it somehow possible for the entire conglomeration to push off against the fist-size contact patch where the tire mashes into the dirt. (Put your fist out and look at it now.) This is asking a lot of that contact patch.

The restarting trick is easy enough on a perfect surface. Any kind of loose aspect to the trail will add heaps of difficulty. The rider must tune into the surface beneath the tire, understand it, match the slope of the hill with a perfect distribution of weight (managing the weight of the head to help control the front tire), and keep the hands, arms, and all the eager upper body muscles thoroughly relaxed. One pedal, foot attached, is ready to go at about two o'clock; the butt is perched on the front of the saddle. Ever so gently the pedal is moved toward the ground—not pushed, but moved. The tires crunch forward, and with the bike still nearly stationary, the second foot is lifted gently from the earth and placed atop its pedal, to increase power as seamlessly as possible in a smooth, round stroke.

This should sound familiar. Classic soft power.

Beginners are stymied by these restarts, failing to understand the soft-power requirements. Freaked out by having to balance at such low speed, they put desperate force into the first pedal stroke and spin out, or tense up, which causes them to yank the bars to the side. We've all been there. Either sort of error turns a restart into a re-stop.

It is a mistake to think in terms of *holding* the bars straight for a restart. If you have to think about keeping the bars straight, you're doing it wrong. Don't consciously think about directing the bars at all; simply put your hands around the grips as lightly as is reasonably possible and keep all the muscles quiet except those needed for finessing the pedals and holding the right balanced body position—this does not include the handlebar-yanking muscles. With those extra muscles released, the pedaling force does not reverberate through to the handlebars at all. So, when the pedal goes down, the bike has a chance to go forward instead of over the side of the mountain.

Restarting on a steep hill really is about relaxation more than anything else. Deficiencies in low-speed balance and pedal familiarity viciously undermine a rider's capacity to relax (see page 22). Beginners can experience quantum-leap improvements in all kinds of low-speed situations, by practicing different types of track stands and other balance tricks. An unconscious relationship with the pedal-cleat interface is also something common to advanced riders that greatly increases their chances for a successful restart—not because clipping in or out is so bloody important on its own, but because worrying about it is so distracting.

If restarting is so tricky, what's the dilemma? Why not just walk the rest of the hill? Interesting question.

We're human and undeniably built for walking and running (and maybe a few other things). Lots of us have been out on a steep climb and noticed that our pace, despite our sense of grandeur, isn't too much faster than the speed of the hikers on the same trail. Sometimes, in fact, we might have a hiker or two waiting for us to get the heck out of their way if we're getting knocked off the pedals on a technical, steep climb. Generally, they are very patient, appreciative of the special effort required by the cyclist on gnarly terrain. "Boy, I respect you guys," they say, waiting as we flounder. And trail runners, forget about it. Mountain biking is faster than running over the course of a whole ride (if the ride includes any real descents), but pedestrians can run past us on steep climbs, if they feel like it. So why ride *any* steep hill?

For one thing, we've got this dang anchor to deal with. If we can't ride a hill, that doesn't mean we can just trot daintily to the top like a fawn. Got to haul the bike too. It's usually easier to ride a trail than it is to walk up the thing while schlepping twenty to thirty awkward pounds off to the side at the same time. Either carrying it or pushing it will be clumsy, and greatly complicated by loose or rough footing. Sometimes the dismounted bike can be used as a sort of walker, a balance aid to lean on, but it will almost always be easier to walk, up or down, without the bike. They call it single-track for a reason. And don't forget the extra time and effort spent climbing on and off the machine, then restarting again, at some point, from zero mph.

So the expert's mode of climbing a trail, by riding it, is usually easier than the beginner's way, of dismounting, hauling, then remounting. Notice the self-reinforcing cycles that are emerging here, as always. The expert keeps rolling, arriving at the top of the hill not only faster but fresher than the struggling beginner. The beginner will have an even tougher time on the next hill after failing to ride this one.

Even if walking with the bike is a little easier, or just as fast, and it sometimes is, this is a mountain bike ride we're on here. Part of the fun of the ride is tackling the technical challenges of the trail—which basically means trying to keep the feet off the ground for long stretches, for the whole ride if possible, as the rocks and roots and slope challenge our skills. Not walking. It's a big part of what mountain biking *is*.

Having to walk sections that others ride can erode the enjoyment of the whole endeavor. In some cases, it can be a little embarrassing or humiliating; it might even keep some people from trail riding again after they've tried it once or twice and experienced mostly frustration.* For many reasons, riding is better than walking, so the ability to restart is very helpful.

Everybody walks their bike up the trail occasionally. Being forced to hike on a mountain bike ride also comes with some hidden advantages: It builds strength and character in a different way than you're used to, and adds variety. Better still, it might indicate that you are getting seriously adventurous in an extraordinary and pristine area. Such areas tend to be not only damn steep, but *empty,* as the majority of riders avoid trails with significant amounts of unrideable terrain.

THE TETRIS ANALOGY In the mid-1980s a Russian computer programmer named Alexey Pazhitnov created a video game called Tetris which, in its clever simplicity, would become one of the most popular and addictive games of all time. Of course, Pazhitnov never made much money off this game, but it made millions for companies like Microsoft, Atari, and Nintendo. In Pazhitnov's game various shapes appear at the top of the screen and move downward, one by one. The player must figure out how and where to stack the object before it reaches the bottom. In the meantime, another shape has appeared at the top and is moving down. The Tetris player succeeds by thinking ahead, looking at the next object as early as possible, and devising a plan on what to do with it. As the game progresses and gets tougher, of course, the objects appear and fall faster, giving the player less time to think.

You see where I'm going with this. The mental process involved in Tetris is quite a bit like the mental process involved in mountain bike trail

---

* Riding with folks who are much more experienced and skillful is the fastest way to learn, but it's easier on the psyche to go out with riders of similar ability. Back in the Day we were all a bunch of rookies, and we stood around by the side of the trail encouraging each other, saying things like "Way to go!" and "Looking good!" (Yeah, this could be more than a little annoying.) Whenever we failed to ride a section, the normal reaction was to go back and try it again, and riding trails became a sort of group effort. Eventually the novelty of riding a bike on rough trails wore off, along with a good deal of the camaraderie. Now there are a lot of riders who are just too cool for school, which for beginners becomes a barrier to entry, as it is in other sports, and riders seem much less likely to turn around and try a section again.

riding. Just like the Tetris player, the trail rider is continuously looking up at the "top of the screen," at the next feature or turn, and devising a plan to deal with it. As the mountain biker speeds up, the obstacles and technical problems drop faster through the field of vision. Like the Tetris player, the trail rider's success depends largely on his or her ability to plan quickly and confidently and move on to the next problem. Strangely, Frogger never taught us much about surviving in traffic, but Tetris can teach us a little something about riding trails.

A 2009 research study found increases in gray matter in the frontal lobes of adolescent girls who played Tetris every day for three months.[33] Trail riding is a sort of puzzle as well, which will surely result in interesting physical changes in a brain that becomes engrossed in it. Visual processing, eye-hand coordination, balance, and problem-solving ability will be trained and strengthened with each ride, just like the muscles.

HAZARD FIXATION Almost every mountain biker, along with just about every motorcyclist and skier, has been advised not to look at objects they want to avoid. *If you look at that tree, you'll run right into it.* While this is an adequate description of just what is likely to happen should a rider become momentarily fixated on an obstacle, it doesn't explain *why* this happens, and so gives beginners few clues to help them understand and conquer this troubling dynamic, commonly known as "target fixation."

As motorcycle-racing instructor Keith Code describes it, target fixation is "where you look at an object you don't want to hit, then become so fixated on the threat that you *don't look for a way out* and hit it anyway."[35] Code has summed up the phenomenon fairly concisely, but right away we can see that the term "target fixation" doesn't really fit, a target being something that you aim for on purpose and actually want to hit.

> But when the ship was within the sound of a man's shout from the land, we fleeing swiftly on our way, the Sirens espied the swift ship speeding toward them, and they raised their clear-toned song:
>
> "Hither, come hither, . . ."
>
> —Homer, *The Odyssey*[34]

Weirdly focused on the obstacle—the anti-target—rather than the target, the two-wheeled version is better termed "hazard fixation."*

That hazard fixation is such a huge theme for motorcyclists and road bikers cornering on smooth surfaces should be an indication of how important it might be for trail riders navigating a rock-strewn and relatively chaotic course. To understand how hazard fixation plays out for the mountain biker, first embrace the basic premise that you only have so much attention to project at the trail ahead of you. To ride good lines on a typical singletrack, you need to direct this limited attention to finding and riding those lines. That is, you need to look where you want or need to go, decide how you want or need to get there, and get there, as the ever-changing terrain continuously scrolls toward you. *Look, decide, ride.*

Should you, while engaged in this process, become preoccupied with a particular nasty feature of the trail—to spice things up, let's call it a cliff-like edge leading to a deep precipice with skeletons and broken bicycles piled at the bottom—should you come around a corner and see this edge, be somewhat surprised by it, and start to consider the prospect of doing a Wile E. Coyote maneuver over it, all this can steal attention from what you had been doing before that, naturally, which was finding the right lines. So, in that crucial split second when your eyes and brain need to be working together to figure out how to get around the corner and down the trail, you will instead be looking elsewhere, and your bike will be rocking and rolling—careening—aimlessly toward the dreaded abyss.

The bike is headed toward the hazard not so much because the rider's eyes are pointed there (although that doesn't help one bit), but because that is the direction the bike happened to be rolling when the rider blacked out and forgot what he was doing. Just a split second is all it takes. The brain freezes, the bike keeps a-rollin'. As the rider awakens to this faulty vector it causes greater alarm and increased fixation on the hazard, which is now even closer and more threatening, which leads to still more wrong-way careening and so on.

---

* Legend has it that the term "target fixation" originated with fighter pilots in the world wars. They would squint and stare down at their targets so intently that they would forget to fly their planes, in some cases riding them right into the ground; they would work so hard to maneuver behind an enemy plane that they would forget about the other enemies buzzing around their own backsides. Now that's true target fixation.

As a final insult, recognition of the rapidly approaching endgame causes the panicked beginner to unleash a last-ditch grab at the brakes, locking the wheels. With traction entirely broken on dirt, the bike is likely to continue in the same direction and at the same speed (or greater) that caused the rider to panic in the first place. Even a little bit of braking will make it more difficult to turn the bike; a lot of braking could make it nearly impossible. At this point the seed of panicked thought is about to be realized as an actual full-fledged disaster. "What you fear is what you find," so it's been said by many a wise uncle or grandma.

And that solves at least some of the mystery of how mountain bikers are seemingly hypnotized and lured in by the very rocks and edges they want to avoid. It's a *disconnect* in the righteous communication between trail and rider, not a particularly intense episode of communication, as it seems at the time.

We've seen that mountain biking is largely about cycles, vicious and virtuous. Hazard fixation is one of the vicious cycles, in which bad technique or mistakes foster worse technique and more mistakes. An experienced rider can recognize the cycle, bust it, and *turn it around* in time to continue on without an incident. There are no Sirens sweetly singing, luring mountain bikers into the rocks. There are no Star Trek "tractor beams" inside our eyes, forcing us to roll toward wherever our eyes are pointed. Hazard fixation is encased entirely between the rider's ears, and in that sense it's entirely within the rider's power to recognize and tame it.

THE WORKOUT Obviously this isn't the best book for you if you're looking for scientific explanations of the physiology of mountain biking, or want specific training programs laid out and things like that. For these subjects, try *Serious Cycling* by Ed Burke, *The Cyclist's Training Manual* by Guy Andrews and Simon Doughty, or some of the many other detailed sources available.

I won't claim to have a firm grasp of the science of exercise. It's freaky stuff when you get into it. The scientists are still working it out, furiously shuffling around their laboratories with large beakers and flasks. The more they look, the more complex it becomes, like most biological processes. While I don't even own a lab coat, I have done an absurd amount of cycling, on the road and trail, and I'm well acquainted with the various physical tortures and joys that mountain biking places on the body.

It's a very, very demanding—and correspondingly rewarding—workout. Climbing a steep hill on a bicycle on rough, loose ground is among the most strenuous, energy-intensive activities available to a human being. The vast majority of humans—the vast majority of cycling enthusiasts—want none of it. Perhaps something like a mixed martial arts or wrestling match would be more strenuous. Really intense hockey or basketball. Skiing up a mountain with a backpack full of rocks. Smashing boulders with a sledgehammer, as fast as possible. Something like that might compare. It takes a bit of doing to provoke such intense exertion. Many serious mountain bike racers shy away from hilly trail rides while training, preferring (or required by coaches) to do much of their training on the road, where their level of effort will be much easier to control and keep within the allotted zones.

For trail riding, both muscular strength and cardiovascular fitness are important. Both endurance and explosive power are important.[36] We've discussed the heck out of how relaxation and balance are important, for both power and technique. Trail riding is full-body exercise, requiring not only leg strength, but strength of the core muscles, especially those deep in the abdomen. There are effective ways to train the mountain bike muscles when off the bike. Many top racers do regular weight training for the thighs and glutes. The best method of strengthening the more obscure of the specialized mountain biking muscles, some of which you never knew you had, is to get out and ride some trails, then ride some more. Yes, relaxation is crucial, but relaxation does not mean muscle *weakness*.

Which is more important for the mountain biker, power or skill? That's a tough one. It depends largely on the terrain. An extra-strong rider doesn't need so much skill. An extra-skillful rider doesn't need so much power. Great trail riders possess both attributes in large quantities.

Since hill climbing is the predominant scenario in cross-country, gravity is the primary adversary, and strength-to-weight ratio is the predominant physical parameter.* Extra fat and bulk won't help on a climb, that's for sure. Hill climbing is the little guy's revenge. When the terrain flattens out, it's no longer about fighting gravity but about fighting air resistance, so the most important physical parameter switches from watts-per-kilogram to watts-per-unit of rider frontal surface area—big folks rock on the flats and suffer mightily on the climbs, is all that means.

Which is more important when climbing hills, leg strength or good lungs? It certainly seems like the muscles depend on the lungs more than the lungs depend on the muscles. Most of the work performed by the legs depends on the ability of the lungs and heart to deliver oxygen to the muscles, where the oxygen reacts with carbs, fats, and proteins to create the fuel that muscles burn (adenosine triphosphate, or ATP); among the by-products of this process is carbon dioxide, which must be pumped away from the muscles and blown out of the body through the lungs. The muscles work admirably without oxygen, but only for a short time. Big lungs for big climbs. Don't be afraid to breathe hard while climbing—your muscles need it. Your lungs are the intake and the exhaust. Think not only about inhaling deeply, but also about exhaling thoroughly to evacuate all the CO_2, to make room for more O_2 deep in the nooks and crannies of the lungs, where it filters into the bloodstream. When the legs start to burn, often a few very thorough exhalations and deep inhalations will be enough to cause noticeable and immediate relief.

When you first start mountain biking, typically the heart and lungs can't keep up, and this causes burning in the legs as well as a feeling of general illness throughout the body. Like the leg muscles, however, the cardiovascular system adapts quickly. Just a few strenuous rides will create

---

* A 2002 study published in the *Journal of Sports Science* compared the physiological characteristics of mountain bikers and road racers, although with a small sample size: "The mountain bikers were lighter (65.3+/-6.5 vs. 74.7+/-3.8 kg, P= 0.01; mean +/- s) and leaner than the road cyclists (sum of seven skinfolds: 33.9+/-5.7 vs. 44.5+/-10.8 mm, P = 0.04). The mountain bikers produced higher power outputs relative to body mass at maximal exercise (6.3+/-0.5 vs. 5.8+/-0.3 W x kg(-1), P= 0.03), at the lactate threshold (5.2+/-0.6 vs. 4.7+/-0.3 W x kg(-1), P= 0.048), and during the 30 min time-trial (5.5+/-0.5 vs. 4.9+/-0.3 W x kg(-1), P = 0.02). Similarly, peak oxygen uptake relative to body mass was higher in the mountain bikers (78.3+/-4.4 vs. 73.0+/-3.4 ml x kg(-1) x min(-1), P = 0.03). The results indicate that high power-to-weight characteristics are important for success in mountain biking. The mountain bikers possessed similar anthropometric and physiological characteristics to previously studied road cycling uphill specialists."[37]

noticeable improvement, as your body builds capillaries in the lungs and legs for more efficient transport of those essential molecules. If you're a beginner who feels overwhelmed by the physical pain of riding trails, know this: If you keep plugging away without overdoing it, and get adequate rest, your body will respond in spectacular fashion.

Unless you're a high-level racer or want to become one, there's no need to overthink nutrition and training. Mountain biking uses a lot of energy, and so requires a lot of quality fuel. The energy derived from food and used in exercise can be expressed in kilocalories (commonly and mistakenly known as calories). Depending on the weight of the rider and level of exertion, a trail rider could burn somewhere between 500 and 1,000 kilocalories per hour. Yes, that's a lot. Off the bike, avid trail riders need to eat a hearty, balanced diet with carbohydrates, protein, and unsaturated fat; include plenty of colorful fruits and vegetables.

On the bike, there's an art to determining just how much food to bring, and what kinds. Use trial and error to find out what works well for you. Avoid riding on a full stomach. After the ride, refuel with gusto so the body can repair itself and grow stronger for the next outing. Since trail riding consumes so much energy, mountain bikers get to eat a little extra pizza later on to make up for it. (And one could easily lose weight by consuming a normal amount of food while doing a lot of trail riding.)

Another critical aspect is hydration. Drink before you get thirsty. Don't skimp on water. Drink liberally on the trail and plenty after the ride as well. Look for signs of dehydration (dark-colored urine, headaches) and quash it with water, water, water. (*Note:* Drinking alcohol after the ride will exacerbate dehydration, because it shuts down the kidneys' system of reabsorbing water back into the bloodstream; instead, it just gets peed out.)

Rest is very important. Don't do hard trail rides every day. Give yourself at least a few days off during the week to recover. Get a lot of quality sleep. For those training or otherwise looking for marked improvements from hard workouts, remember that rest is a key component of any training program, equal with the workouts. Only with rest can the muscles and stressed systems repair themselves and become stronger; otherwise, they just get more and more beaten down.

Watch closely for signs of overtraining, or, if you don't consider yourself to be training, over-riding: high resting heart rate, burning in the leg muscles at the drop of a hat, irritability, getting sick too easily, and a feeling of just plain not wanting to ride. Failing to heed the signs of overtraining would be disastrous for a racer's form, for a long time. Many if not most young racers, in their exuberance and inexperience, get to learn about the vagaries of overtraining firsthand.

TOO MUCH Trail riding can be so strenuous, so exhausting— so painful—there is definitely an element of masochism involved. Self-torture. As cross-country fiends we are disappointed if the ride brings no pain, or insufficient amounts. More than once I have heard (and used myself) the darker language of Judeo-Christian religious traditions to describe the pain of a long climb, and our relationship to it: We go into the mountains to "suffer for our sins." This is more than a devotion to exercise. What are we looking for out there? Perhaps the better question is, what are we running from?

In addition to being a little creepy, the trail rider's quest for pain can cause long-term health issues. It's simply not true that all pain turns to gain. We tend to assume that the harder we ride, the better we will become—stronger, faster, healthier. But at some point, it's just too much. Though it may be difficult for longtime cyclists to accept, raging up a climb with the heart beating out of the chest is not necessarily an activity that is conducive to a long, healthy life.

Consider the pattern of mortality among old bike racers. Anecdotally, a disturbing number of former top-level riders seem to die with heart issues in their fifties and sixties. It's tempting to ascribe this to the frenzied ingestion of performance-enhancing drugs that has been going on since the early days of the sport, and many insiders do, but researchers suspect that the hyperexertion alone can damage the heart in some nasty ways. [38]

Although their results do not prove a causal relationship between endurance sports and RV [right ventricular] involvement or allow conclusions about the risk of sudden death in this population, "this risk is definitely higher than expected from data in general athlete populations," Heidbüchel et al write. Due to the high prev-

alence of RV involvement in the study group, they suspect not only that endurance training triggers arrhythmias in athletes with preexisting arrhythmogenic RV dysplasia but also that "endurance sport by itself may have contributed to the RV structural and electrical modifications." Mont and Brugada agree, suggesting that high-performance endurance sports may lead to structural RV changes, which can cause a "kind of 'acquired right ventricular dysplasia' that may finally produce ventricular arrhythmias and sudden death," adding, "excessive endurance training may have deleterious consequences for the heart," a relationship that needs to be confirmed by larger, case-control studies. Doping agents, which recently have been detected in routine doping tests in a number of top-level cyclists, are known to increase the risk of cardiac mortality and may also play a role in the development of arrhythmias.[39]

That puts a new twist on it, eh?

This needs to be considered in the larger context. Even with this complication, endurance athletes still live a lot longer, are a lot less likely to die suddenly of a heart attack, than sedentary people. Don't stop riding.

Just ease up a little bit, if you can allow yourself the luxury. Mountain biking can be really, really good for you, very effective exercise, but take care with prolonged bouts of *extreme* exertion.

A GOOD TRAIL WILL ERASE YOUR BRAIN

Every year my wife goes up and does a hilly century ride around Aspen to benefit a breast cancer foundation. My strategy regarding this fact is simple: I stash myself and my mountain bike in her car right before she leaves. By the time she discovers this extraneous cargo, it's generally too late to turn back.

It is late summer in 2010 and we're spending the night up at Snowmass, at a hotel called the Wildwood Inn. I've stayed here multiple times over the years. I liked the Wildwood a lot more before I found out that Ted Bundy abducted one of his victims, Caryn Campbell, from the second-floor hallway in January 1975.* That knowledge will cast a pall over my future relations with the resort.

Snowmass is a collection of big hotels in a beautiful green mountain valley not far from Aspen. A ski resort, of course. While some of Colorado's resorts are attached to actual towns that have been around since the mining booms of the 1800s (Aspen, Crested Butte, Silverton, Breckenridge, Telluride), others are entirely prefab, created from scratch in the second half of the twentieth century. Snowmass is one of these, Vail another. Note that the central areas of each of these resorts is named "village." Snowmass Village, Vail Village. The old mining towns like Crested Butte don't have to try to evoke that cozy cutesiness. With the rows of sharp-roofed Victorian houses and the preserved Old West saloons, it's already there. Strangely, the new resorts didn't try to copy the pleasing tableau of the vintage Colorado mining town. They shot straight back to the Old World with their fakery, going for a Swiss Alpine sort-of-thing. There are a lot of places called *haus* and innumerable Bavarian *fachwerk* "chalets" with fake cobblestone driveways.

Snowmass, Vail, Aspen—it's all great by me. Incredible trail rides abound from any of those locations.

---

* The story of Bundy in Colorado is a particularly ugly part of the state's history. He murdered at least three women around the state (there were murders in Snowmass, Vail, and Grand Junction to which he admitted, plus one in Golden and one along the Peak-to-Peak Highway near Nederland to which he is linked by strong circumstantial evidence). After being arrested and hauled back here to stand trial for Campbell's murder in 1977, Bundy leaped from a second-story window of the county courthouse in Aspen and ran a few blocks to the Roaring Fork River, rearranged his clothes, then strolled nonchalantly through town and escaped. He walked to the base of the ski area and hiked up and over the mountain as the police set up roadblocks and called in the dogs.

Bundy was carrying maps of the area and was apparently looking for the Pearl Pass Road to Crested Butte, where the sport of mountain biking was, at that very moment, being brewed from drunken attempts to ride huge passes on one-speed "klunkers." (The first Crested Butte-to-Aspen ride/party had taken place the previous September.) Bundy never found Pearl Pass, or was scared from its heights by late spring snow, and the women of Crested Butte were spared.

Bundy wandered in the woods around Castle Creek for nearly a week, breaking into cabins. Finally he went back to the edge of Aspen and stole an old Cadillac that had been left with the keys inside. Driving erratically in a semiconscious daze, he was stopped and recaptured almost immediately by the Aspen police. It should have ended there. Awaiting trial again, Bundy escaped from the Glenwood Springs jail in December 1977, by leaving his law books under the blankets on his bunk and squirming out a 1-foot-square hole he had hacksawed into the ceiling. He boarded a plane in Denver and landed in Chicago before his absence was noticed, and went on to Florida to continue killing. He was arrested in Florida in 1979 and executed in 1985.[40]

When you've got Ted Bundy or similar modern horrors on the brain, a proper singletrack trail is one of the few things out there that can wipe these polluting thoughts away. And the Government Trail is about as proper as it gets. Hanging high over the Brush Creek valley, about 1,000 feet over the Snowmass resort, the Government stretches pretty much all the way to Aspen on one end and up into the watery crook of the high mountain valley on the other. The primary attitude of this contouring singletrack is fast, rolling. There are maybe ten or fifteen singletrack trails in the West that have burned themselves onto my hide, and upon which I am constantly wishing and imagining myself, and this is one of them.

If I just head straight up the ski slope I'll find it. But it's no easy task getting there. It'll be about twenty or thirty solid minutes of huffing, basically straight up. Thirty minutes? Honestly, I don't know. Time does bizarre things when you're near max effort on a slow, steep climb. This direct approach provokes a ridiculous enough workout that I won't need any more exercise for the rest of the week, let alone the rest of the day. I crave it, I need it, I guess. It's important—even fun on some level that I could never explain—but it won't be my favorite aspect of the ride today.

Finding the trail hanging up there as always, I turn onto it and switch from toiling to floating. The trail flashes in and out of the trees as it crosses the ski slopes, alternating light and black. Into the forest the trail is deep black, soft living soil. Humified. Green shoots hurl themselves out of the moist dirt toward the sky—new trees, new ferns and grasses everywhere. The trail would disappear under a green sea within days, if not for an occasional ripping encounter with a mountain bike tire or hiking boot.

The forest on this side of the valley is lush and thick, difficult to walk through. The undergrowth is made of broad leaves that are always wet when you get off the bike to piss or crawl into the bushes to hide from your riding partners. This is the improbably dank, chilled world of the north-facing slope in the Rocky Mountains. Over on the opposite side of the valley, it's a completely different scene. Scrub oak and cactus cling to a harsh dry ridge made of shale, nuked by the sun. Peering out at the south-facing side from beneath my parasol of fluttering aspen, dry death appears to own the inside track over there. Having been on that side a few times, I know it's a bit of an optical illusion.

While some singletracks are remembered for singular features, like a long uphill grind (Barr Trail) or unique geology (Slickrock), trails like the Government are defined by their delicious variation, dabbling in a wide array of modes with quick changes between them. The constant engagement of the rider on the Government Trail, dipping and diving around trunks of aspen and blue spruce, rocking over the associated roots, long gliding traverses on hardpack at speed—and now comes a switchback, a stream crossing, a lurching move up and over a pile of rock—it's therapeutic. A little of this, little of that, and never a dull moment.

On such a trail the masterful rider spends a great deal of time hovering over the seat, moving the bike and body in response to and (better) anticipation of the ever-changing geometry of the surface and objects scattered across it. Finessing the brakes, frequently changing gears, readjusting both lines, and always looking forward, forward. As speeds ramp up, so do the demands of the Government. Riding a trail like that involves a staggeringly huge amount of little decisions that have to be made in a very short period of time, or are made somehow for us, it's impossible to say. If the rider hopes to stay on the bike and keep rolling from section to section, piecing it all together, the looking, assessing, decision making, and body movement never stops.

Concentration on the scrolling series of tasks at hand means, among other things, that the nagging stresses of the real world are squeezed out of the rider's conscious mind, by necessity. There is no room for anything but trail. But not only that—the blood runs to the legs, the jaw and face muscles slacken, the miracle of balance tickles the inner ear, endorphins (think *endogenous morphine*) and other mysterious opiate- and cannabinoid-like chemicals pulse from various glands into the bloodstream as effort increases.*All of these facets of the ride contribute to

---

* Exercise-induced analgesia (pain relief) is a well-studied phenomenon. Much of the research has centered around a type of technique called "noxious stimulation," described in the following passage: "A number of investigators have studied changes in pain perception following cycling exercise using noxious dental pulp stimulation techniques. For example, Pertovaara et al. assessed changes in dental pain thresholds during and following exercise at different intensities. Dental pain thresholds were determined with a Bofors Pulp Tester, in which a cathode was attached to an upper tooth, and assessments were completed before, during and following exercise. Four different levels of exercise (50, 100, 150 and 200W) were completed on a bicycle ergometer by 6 men. Workloads were increased stepwise without rest between the different levels, and each work period lasted 8 minutes. It was reported that dental pain thresholds tended to increase with the increasing workloads. However, a significant increase in pain thresholds was only evident at the 200W workload. Dental pain thresholds remained elevated 30 minutes following exercise."[41]

a strong trance-like effect on the trail rider's brain. The term "runner's high" doesn't adequately describe the mountain biker's dream state, in which the technical aspects of riding the bike, the never-ending decisions made in partnership with the trail, consume the operator's available attention. It's no surprise that many stressed-out mountain bikers find "trail trance" to be quite a soothing, if not outright intoxicating, state of mind. To some of us, it may even be the main attraction.

The Government is one of the most trancey trails I've ever been on. Frankly, I could ride back and forth on the thing all day long and be happy. No, not happy—in a state of bliss. But today I want to get across to the other side of the valley as well and ride the trail that roller-coasters along the top of that north-facing ridge, and loop back to the start. It seems like an obvious loop, and I'm sure locals do versions of it all the time. I've been drooling over the idea for years. So I surfed the Government for a while then bombed down to its terminus in the dark corner of the valley above the resort and popped out onto a road.

At this point, of course, I turned the wrong way and started rolling down Snowmass Creek away from the resort, which is in the valley of *Brush Creek*. Hey, it seemed right, and I'm in a trance, remember? By the time I figured out my mistake, I had already descended a few miles down the wrong road, so I thought, heck, I'll keep on rolling down and look for a way up the ridge from this side. I had a map that showed some promising roads that might take me up onto the ridge.

My ride then took an ominous and ugly turn as the dirt road turned to asphalt. The lines on the map turned out to be roads to nowhere, if nowhere can be defined as a place with no singletrack but lots of driveways, each of which sports a multimillion-dollar summer home on one end and a bright blue Apex Security placard on the other. I've seen this movie before and it doesn't end well; the death of a trail ride, the end of the trance.

It pays to know exactly where you're going and how to get there. (I was about to write that it's a good idea to have a local along to show the way, but then I remembered all the supposedly knowledgeable locals who'd presided over haplessly wandering groups over the years.) Getting lost can be good if it opens the door to finding new trails and learning more about a certain area. If it *shortens* your ride, it's no good whatsoever.

Eventually I made it back to the ski mountain and its web of trails, but the spell was broken. Next year. Next year, I'll ride that loop.

CONFIDENCE AND FEAR

Confidence is definitely part of the Virtuous Cycle, there with relaxation, breathing, flow. But it is not something that can be taught, manipulated. Confidence comes when it comes. Confidence happens when it's ready. You can't force or manufacture genuine confidence in any way other than real on-the-bike experience, over time.

> **"**
> Fear happens. It is what it is.
> **—Dave**[42]

There is a tendency to put the cart before the horse regarding confidence. Beginning riders often experience a distinct lack of confidence—a great deal of fear—in certain situations on the trail. They can see that their friends don't have the same "mental block." Sometimes they think they can mind-warp or somehow self-hypnotize out of this fear and into a state of confidence.

A mistake beginners often make is to assume that the fear itself is the primary thing standing in the way of a high level of prowess. In other words, beginners may delude themselves that they really are good at this, that they just need to clear some pesky mental furniture in order to unleash their innate mountain biking ability. This is a very *impatient* interpretation of the fear.

Let's look inside the brain of the expert trail rider for a moment. It's pretty messy in there, but right away we can see that something is missing. Expert trail riders ride *without fear*. This can be easily misunderstood. I am not advising anyone to strive to ride without fear, as that would be bad advice.

The sense of well-being, the absence of fear, enjoyed by the expert trail rider is like a gauge that indicates everything is running well with the machine to which the gauge is attached. If the gauge starts to move into the red, we do not say "Let's jimmy with that gauge, Bart, then the machine will get better." We know we have to fix the machine, whatever is causing the gauge to go red.

Gauges start to scream trouble when a mountain biker, at that point in time, doesn't fully know what he or she is doing, and realizes it. When the rider enters this unknown territory, alarm bells ring left and right. And they should. Rigging or unplugging the alarms won't somehow cure the rider's deficit of skill and experience. Someone who rides both beyond critical abilities and without fear will get slammed to the ground repeatedly until the lesson sinks in. I have known a few people like that over the years.

Interestingly, we learn not to equate fear with a heightened state of awareness. Not only are these very different things, they are mutually exclusive. It is impossible to ride well in a fearful state, because worry and preoccupation disrupt our awareness by interrupting the stream of trail-processing thoughts. This stream of thought is not terribly complex, but it must be continuous. In this way fear becomes self-fulfilling prophecy. But again, this does not mean fear should be banished or destroyed, or quietly swept under a cerebral cortex somewhere. *Fear is not the problem.* The problem is the rider, rolling faster than his or her capacity to process information effectively.

Once the fearful novice practices for a while and makes some sense of things, the fear dissipates for legitimate reasons, without any need to will or trick it away, without noticing it go; what is left after the fear dissipates is called confidence. Real trail confidence is a non-feeling, a complete calm that comes from understanding one's abilities and riding within them.

MOJO WORKIN' When the electrified bluesman Muddy Waters sang in 1957 about his "mojo" and how it was "workin'," it wasn't a thinly veiled reference to the male sexual apparatus, as many assume. Mojo is magic, voodoo. If your mojo is workin', it means the ladies are under your spell. I wonder how Muddy would feel if he knew that some phantom trail surfer up in Colorado was using "Got My Mojo Workin'" in the twenty-first century, to induce within himself an optimal state for riding his bicycle on mountain trails, as the trees fly by in a blur.* I'm guessing he would be a little bemused.

* According to most sources, McKinley Morganfield, known as Muddy Waters, heard somebody else perform "Got My Mojo Workin'" then tried to copyright the song as his own, perhaps changing it slightly. There has been a lot of litigation and controversy over the song's origins. According to one court decision, "MOJO is a commonplace part of the rhetoric of the culture of a substantial portion of the American people. As a figure of speech, the concept of having, or not having, one's MOJO working is not something in which any one person could assert originality, or establish a proprietary right."[43] That's good to know.

"Got My Mojo Workin' " really isn't a very positive song, if you listen to the whole thing. The mojo is workin', yes, but it *don't work* on the specific object of Muddy's mojo overtures, whoever she is. *Got my mojo workin', but it don't work on you.* It's actually a little depressing. So I leave that part out: Got my mojo workin', period. When I'm singing that part of the song out on the singletrack (my singletrack soundtrack), the mojo is just plain working, no strings attached, no qualifications. So in my head it goes a little something like this:

Got my mojo workin' (Got my mojo workin')
Got my mojo workin' (Got my mojo workin')

That's the heart of Muddy's song. Immediately, I start riding well. My mojo, it starts a-workin', as if called out of the dirt and into my soul. The tension flows out of my body and dissipates into the air. (I think that's where it goes.) Instead of negotiating the trail's obstacles, I am dancing with the whole thing, its secret flow revealed. My tires slide into the turn—all part of the dance. My body knows what to do, doesn't seem to be receiving signals from the brain anymore, but from some other source. I am one with the earth, its trees, rocks, and dirt. I am trail riding like a freakin' champ. Not sure how I got this song in my head in the first place, years ago, but singing a little "Mojo Workin' " has been one of the most effective strategies I have ever employed, in any aspect of life.

It's highly doubtful that singing "Mojo Workin' " will have the same amazing effect on you that it has on me. But there might be some other song or phrase that works for you in a similar way. Most of these phrases tend to be three, four words, maybe six or seven words at most. I think it has to be pretty short, so you don't have to think about the phrase itself very much at all—just enough. One trail rider I know simply repeats the words "Play it cool, [her last name]" when she starts to tighten up, and swears it's very effective. That's right to the point. She listens to herself. Another friend silently jams MC Hammer's "Can't Touch This," with its infective Rick James groove.* "Can't touch this" and "got my mojo workin'" are nice positive (somewhat presumptuous) reassurances, but they're a lot more than that. They're music. The beauty of repeating such a phrase of a song could be in its rhythm and rhythm-inducing powers. It turns the ride into a dance, which is just about what it should be.

Repeating a mantra, chant, or song might also work by calming the thoughts as well as the muscles. With a simple phrase running through the mind, the distracting chatter is displaced. The human mind does not have the ability to deal effectively with more than one thought at the same time. Worries and distractions banished, only the benign song remains, and the musty folds of the brain are cleared to process the upcoming trail features, the feedback from the bike, the sounds—a huge amount of useful information if the mind is open to it, and not covered in a shell of distraction.

Or, the mojo that's workin' might just be pure placebo effect—I believe it'll help, so it does. For whatever reason, putting the sing in singletrack does the trick for me.

THE DRAGON AND THE DIRT Many of the people I've ridden trails with over the years were highly experienced urban cyclists—street cyclists. Every last one of these folks would tell you, without any hesitation, they feel safer on the trail than on the street. Even though crashing is not an infrequent occurrence on the dirt, the impossibility of serious smash-ups with cars and trucks overwhelms other considerations. To these veteran commuters and ex-messengers, singletrack offers an especially attractive sort of freedom and power. Freedom from the mistakes of others, power over one's own destiny. It's refreshing.

---

* This kind of thing is also common in the sports that are cousin to mountain biking. In *Skiing: The Mind Game*, Marlin MacKenzie writes, "The internal auditory information processed by expert skiers almost always consists of short positive statements or commands. Ben-Henry Jones, a senior skier, praises himself regularly when he skies well. He silently asserts, 'Good. Good.' . . . Chris Parrot, a former U.S. Junior Olympic competitor in all the alpine events, sings a 1965 Beatles tune, 'If I Fell In Love With You,' in his head; the rhythm of the tune matches the rhythm of his turns."[44]

Almost all kinds of car–bike collisions can be avoided by a cyclist who is tuned in to the surroundings.* But the hits-from-behind, not so much. Even the most defensive and experienced rider is, to some unavoidable degree, at the mercy of drivers approaching from behind. With respect to these strangers, the cyclist's presence on the road is something of an act of faith—that this guy who is about to pass isn't reaching down to fiddle with his radio/navigation unit/DVD player/everything at the wrong moment.

Thus a dark cloud of uncertainty hangs over every street cyclist, even the most careful among them. An old messenger friend called it "The Dragon," that which can swoop down out of nowhere and take you out. He had an image of it tattooed on his arm. Thankfully, almost all drivers possess the minimum awareness necessary to avoid a bicyclist who is in front of them and plainly visible, or else nobody could ride on the street.

On the trail, the dark cloud disappears. Nothing will randomly take you out while trail riding, with the possible exception of a very hungry mountain cat, or a charging moose. Dirt slays the dragon.

CASUALTIES How's this for a scientific hypothesis: If mountain bikers were dropping like flies, or even like on-road bikers, we would know about it. Not to be dismissive or disrespectful of those who have paid the ultimate price for their singletrack, because surely there have been some. But that number, whatever it is, would almost certainly be considered very small by any reasonable observer. There seems to be only a scattering. Finding the actual number would probably be impossible, due to the way the deaths are classified, or rather, not classified.

Even though every trail rider on the planet has wrecked at some point, I'd never heard of anybody actually dying from a mountain bike crash until I went a-googling on the subject. Informal flipping through a pile of random news reports from the past few decades seems to indicate that a substantial percentage of fatalities pinned on mountain biking are actually due to heart attacks. Trail riding can be very hard on the heart, no

---

* The bulk of car-bike collisions involve some sort of turning or crossing by one or both parties—bicyclist pulls out in front of car, car turns left into bicyclist, etc. Hits from behind, while relatively infrequent, are also disproportionately deadly. Around one-quarter of all cyclist fatalities involve hits from behind.[45]

doubt. Among those who died in actual crashes—and there doesn't seem to be very many of those at all, considering that an estimated eight million or so people went mountain biking at least once during 2010 (according to the industry)—many seem to have ridden off a cliff. Dramatic. Ever have that dream? Locations where such a tragedy could occur are limited. Most are well-known, like the famous Portal Trail, on the edge of a sheer sandstone cliff near Moab. One spot on the Portal, if you happen to catch a pedal on one modest but critically placed toaster-shaped rock, you're gone. It's not a particularly difficult move; a lot of people go for it, and not all of them make it.

Professional mountain bike racer Beth Coates was killed in 1996—in a rock climbing accident in El Dorado Canyon. Now there's a sport with serious consequences. In 2010 at least eleven individuals died while climbing or mountaineering in the big mountains of Colorado. One victim slipped and fell down a glacier. He pulled the rope down with him, and his two companions were left stranded on the slope. That sort of life-and-death dependence on others is rarely a part of the trail-riding scene. We're not that hardcore. And as for skiing—a few years ago Colorado's ski industry was trying to smooth over the negative PR after nearly twenty deaths in a single season. Most of the victims smashed into trees at high speed (with their helmets on).

Studies focusing specifically on mountain bikers' injuries are few and far between. Most of those that do exist look only at racers in competitions, as the start list of a race or race series makes a tidy cohort for study. Not surprisingly, these studies found that racers who are trying to go fast at all times do a fair bit of crashing. Higher injury rates are also associated with other riskier forms of the sport, the freeride stuff, downhilling, dirt jumping, and North Shore–style man-made obstacles, which invite riders to land on their face from 20 feet up.

A research study involving the Vancouver trauma centers that serve the North Shore trails counted all mountain bike injuries in the area from 1992 through 2002. The amount and amplitude of the injuries—impressive carnage. Sixty-six percent of the patients required surgery. Damn. The study also found that the number of injuries was pretty much skyrocketing over that ten-year period, reflecting the growing popularity of a more dangerous form of riding, and greater numbers of riders in that specific area. But get this—only one death was recorded, in ten years of relatively extreme mountain biking on the North Shore.[46] Compared to the bunny slopes of Colorado, it's a total garden party up there.

Despite this lack of casualties, the alleged danger of mountain biking is much celebrated in popular culture. "Overblown" might be a good way to put it.

WHO CRASHES? Everybody.

More specifically, the one who crashes is the one riding, at least in that moment, outside his or her abilities. By definition, you see, it must be so. While that means everybody crashes, at some point or another, very experienced trail surfers can enjoy many thousands of miles of singletrack without a single crash, because they have carved out a very wide domain of control, over many years. But nobody goes through the process of learning to ride trails without at least a few wrecks.

The one riding outside his or her abilities is often the one tagging along with fast (faster), much more experienced friends, trying like hell to keep up. That's a quick way to learn, by closely watching those with better skills. Ultimately, we want to learn by watching other cyclists, not jockeys. Unfortunately, this method can be a little painful at times.

SOME THINGS TO PRACTICE Through

the book so far I've dropped a few tips for beginners on specific drills they can practice to vastly improve their overall experience. To keep them straight, here's a summary:

1. Crawl all over the bike, to get a feel for different points of balance and the importance of relaxation. Practice hard cornering and hard braking with different body action. Feel it, baby. If you have to think about turning and braking, you're not doing it right.

2. Clip in and out until it's absolutely unconscious. The goal is to use the pedals seamlessly without ever thinking about them during the ride.

3. Learn to "track stand" (balance on the bike while it is stationary). Effective for building confidence over technical sections. Learn to track stand stylishly, unconsciously.

4. Learn to do a very small wheelie. Lifting the front wheel onto or over obstacles is a crucial skill.

5. Know basic maintenance and trailside mechanics. Learn to fix a flat and true a wheel. Mess around with your brakes and drivetrain components in order to grasp the basic concept of their function. Learn to manage basic adjustments of these components, and learn how to replace brake pads and chains.

6. Understand your suspension. Try out different settings, learn how to make adjustments on the trail, and clean and maintain the suspension components. Suspension adjustments can have a profound effect on ride quality. No suspension? Great. You're probably much better off in the long run if you learn to ride trails on a rigid fork.

7. Ride a skinny-tired road bike on singletrack trails, or at least on dirt roads. Get a feel for two-wheel drift and hone your vision. Make those fat tires seem *fat*.

PART II

LOGISTICS

WHAT'S IN YOUR PACK? *Wait a minute—do you mean to tell me I have to wear a freaking backpack when I ride trails?* Well, no, you don't have to. With a bit of creativity you can carry the necessary gear in jersey pockets, or a combo of pockets and little pouches attached to the bike, even for some longer rides. Obviously, it depends on the ride: How long is it? How high is it? Have you done it before? What are the weather possibilities? How much water and food do you need to carry? *That's a lot of questions, dude. If I can get away with not wearing a backpack, I'm going to go for it. I'll take my chances.* You got that part right. What if a storm comes in while you're way out there? That Sinbad T-shirt is not going to cut the mustard.

I need to bring a jacket and other bad-weather gear—on every ride? That seems pretty extreme. I bring a waterproof shell and some kind of warm long-sleeve top on pretty much every ride except for those that are really short and close to shelter, but then, the mountains are pretty nutty. Often I'll bring a pair of warm gloves and a hat, along with some tights. It's dangerous to try to predict the weather up there, best just to prepare for whatever. On second thought, scratch that. It's actually impractical to pre-pare in a thorough fashion for a really bad mountain storm. Every time I get caught in one of these things I wish I had more gear on board. Doesn't matter how much I have, I always want more. More thermal layers, thicker gloves and hat, a few more socks, maybe thicker tights—you get the pic-ture. I wish I had a full-on thermal suit, like some kind of ice road mainte-nance worker. This sensation is especially acute at high altitudes, several hours from shelter. There is no perfect preparation up there, not on a bike; there is inadequate, and dangerously inadequate.

You're scarin' me, bro. You might not need any extra clothing for four-teen out of fifteen rides, but when ride number fifteen comes around and you get nailed with something really nasty, snow and sleet over 10,000 feet—and the gear is all there—believe me, it makes up for all those days when you carried the gear but didn't need it. If the storm hits when there's no gear, it's not just annoying. It can be a life-threatening situation. Most likely, you're in for a rather extreme and unpleasant adventure, so bad it will make you pack all kinds of extra gear from that point onward. Notice how the veteran trail riders come prepared.

But I do most of my riding behind the Wal-Mart in Tucson. Oh, okay then. Obviously, clothing requirements will be dictated by the location and length of the ride. Short ride in the desert on a clear day, no jacket required. Likewise, if your ride will be contained in a relatively small area, with easy escapes to shelter, might as well go light as possible. If all your rides are like that though, the extra weight that must be hauled for a so-called *epic* ride will persecute you as much as the ride itself. Getting ready for such adventures includes developing a tolerance for a weighty pack.

My buddies and I are going for a long ride next weekend. Maybe I could make extra room for jackets by leaving all my tools at home. Ah, no, my friend. Carry all the tools you might need to keep your particular bike rolling, within reason. I have (about four sizes of) Allen wrenches, tire levers, patch kit, pump, SRAM master link, chain tool, tiny screwdriver, tiny pliers of some sort, spoke wrench, and electrical tape. (A lot of this stuff could be found on a single multitool.) Often a little bit of lube. Depending on your individual situation, it may be necessary to carry a few specialized pieces. I used to have to carry a little 14-millimeter wrench to adjust my V-brakes, for instance.

I carry some extras too, although rather haphazardly: brake pads, some spokes, a cable. Carrying spares isn't something I get too excited about, although I have found occasion to dig each of those items out of the pack deep into a stupid-long ride. So maybe I should get excited about it, and use a more systematic approach.

Also, take a map of the area trails if such a map is available and meets minimum standards for accuracy (how will you know if it does or doesn't until you get out there and check?). Try to find a dedicated trail map designed and vetted by mountain bikers. A detailed topographic map is best. The ability to read a topographic map is powerful knowledge. A little Bic lighter will provide enough light to let you read the map in the dark, and also comes in handy for starting a fire when you misread the map, get lost, and have to spend the night in the woods. (Another way to read a map in the dark: Take a picture of the map with a digital camera, then zoom in on the image.)

I bring the stuff and encourage others to do the same. It's not like road riding, where you can call a taxi or even flag somebody down. With mountain biking, it's not just that things go wrong, it's that they go wrong while you're deep in the forest, on a mountainside somewhere, or out in the desert. A seemingly tiny lapse in preparation—say, forgetting to bring an inner tube—could have serious consequences. Of course, it probably won't.

If I get a flat or something, can't I just use my buddy's tools? He always carries so much junk-ola in his pack. If your friend is like most mountain bikers, he won't mind helping you out. However, it could happen that a mechanical issue strikes when your buddy isn't in a good position to help. Maybe he's far ahead of you on the trail. So he'll be up there waiting at a trail junction, or at the end of the ride, wondering what the heck. At some point he gets worried and comes back to look for your sorry self (or, perhaps, he just shrugs and drives home). This is the opposite of self-reliance. It's better to carry your own equipment, and to understand how to use it.

Self-reliance was a central concept in mountain biking in the early days of the sport, when adventure and preparedness were valued as much as speed and performance. Cross-country racing developed with an important rule: Any mechanical snafus or flat tires would have to be dealt with by the racer alone, using only the tools with which he or she started the race. That's a throwback to bicycle races of the early twentieth century, which were similar to mountain bike races in many ways. Now imagine how such a rule would put today's Euro peloton into absolute chaos. I get a mental image of fourteen or so extremely aggravated dudes frantically truing their wheels by the side of the road after a big stack-up, swarmed by a crowd of slobbering, shouting, drunken Basques, and it makes me smile. That self-reliant spirit has been fading from mountain bike racing, and perhaps from casual trail riding as well. But there's still a long way to go before mountain biking is as scrubbed of self-reliance as road racing.* Never assume that someone else in the group (see page 88) will bail you out. What if your friend accidentally leaves some of his stuff at home, or you need a different-size spoke wrench or something? Make sure you're covered, by covering yourself.

It's helpful to keep everything in the pack even when you're not riding, if possible. The same basic set of gear for every ride. That way it will always be there ready to go and doesn't have to be gathered from distant corners of the house each time.

All the clothing and tools you mentioned so far barely fit in my pack. Well, you'd better strap it down and stuff it in, because the heaviest, bulkiest items are yet to come.

FOOD AND WATER Prepare for a strenuous trail ride

by eating well the preceding evening (more accurately, the preceding ten years). Eat some sort of breakfast on ride day, but let it digest for an hour or more before starting out. You don't want it sneaking up and saying howdy as you climb the day's first hill.

Typical trail rides last about two hours or so, not enough time to necessitate bringing much food along. For these garden-variety American recreational outings, just an energy bar or two will be fine (unless you get stuck out there for some reason). For rides of four or more hours, you'll have to pack more than a few energy bars and gels. You're going to need, like, a sandwich or something. Maybe two, in addition to the bars and gels. Plus a banana and some pretzels. Real food, in other words. After a few hours of riding, your body will probably be craving the caloric equivalent

---

* The shifting valuation of self-reliance in the sport of mountain biking was highlighted in 2002, when the dominant Canadian racer Roland Green found himself sidelined by a loose cleat at Big Bear, and without any tools in his jersey pocket. He fixed the cleat with a multitool that was tossed to him by a teammate. Green went on to win the race, as he did most races, seemingly, in those days. The violation was seen on television but nobody at the venue noticed it, so there was no protest within the allotted protest period. It seems likely that another racer would have protested if any had seen the violation. The incident sparked debate about sporting ethics and the viability of the old self-reliance rule. Some said that simply borrowing a teammate's tool shouldn't disqualify Green from the win, since he clearly was the strongest rider. Others said What??! He couldn't even carry his own multitool? Then he should have accepted the consequences. The governing body of mountain bike racing in the United States (USA Cycling) added all kinds of loopholes for pro races in 2010, and Green's tool transgression would now be legal.[1] The teammate who tossed the multitool to Green was Ryder Hesjedal.

of a full meal; a few hours after that, it will want another one. That means a few thousand kilocalories in the pack for very long rides.

The energy demands of cross-country trail riding are too intense to keep pedaling through epic-length rides without refueling. Lack of fuel leads to "The Bonk," a physical revolt by the body that makes every pedal stroke a struggle. This is more than just normal fatigue from a tough ride, which probably feels good to you on some level if you're reading this book. "Bonking" is not another term for being uncomfortably tired. It's a profound state of depletion, and you'll recognize it when it occurs.

If you deplete yourself so completely in a semi-wilderness setting, far from the trailhead, it could be somewhat dangerous. It might be a struggle just to get back home. It's not unusual, for instance, for a seriously bonked rider to have to walk every single minor uphill section he encounters, and slowly. It'll turn an ultrastrong, tough guy into a whimpering, shivering noodle. Add a sudden storm, and there could be grave issues. You'll be especially vulnerable to hypothermia. Such an episode can have fairly serious long-term consequences as well, weakening the body and bodily systems, setting overall fitness back a notch or two, and opening the door to illness. Anything that doesn't kill you makes you stronger? Maybe, in the very long term. Bonking is bad.

What I'm saying is, bring enough food.

Water is the most important thing on board, and the heaviest too. *Wait—I have two water bottle cages on my bike. Why am I putting water in my backpack?* Oh, you'll use the cages all right, unless you just prefer to use a hydro-pack (e.g., Camelbak). But for really long rides, you can't carry enough water on the bike. Some more will go on the back, either in a hydro-pack situation or in an extra bottle or two. Alternatively (or additionally), carry a serious water filter and reload from a stream along the route. Don't bank on the presence of running water along an unfamiliar route, even if someone told you it would be there, or even if there's a squiggly blue line on the map. Things change, especially streams, from day to day and year to year. Quite often those little blue lines denote bone-dry arroyos. Stash a few water-purification tablets somewhere in the pack, just in case.

Don't skimp on water. Don't decide to ration yourself to smaller sips so you won't have to carry as much. Ideally, you don't ration yourself at all with water. Water rationing is an answer to a screw-up, not a desirable strategy. For effective riding we need to drink liberally, especially on hot days. If you wait until you're feeling thirsty, you'll get behind on the hydration. If you ration yourself to a sip when you need big gulps, you'll hurt yourself in the short and long term. Dehydration is as damaging as the Bonk.

Your well-prepared pack will be noticeably heavy at this point. About ten pounds is typical, could be more. This weight works against us as we try to negotiate the trail, no doubt about it. Smaller riders will be more aggrieved by it. Anyone who isn't used to it will dislike it. The pack weight must be understood and managed in the same way we manage the weight of our heads (see page 14). But everything in there is important. You have to bring it, even if you probably won't need most of it. Luckily it works out that we need more water on days when we require less bad-weather gear, and vice versa, which tempers the weight a bit.

As you start sucking down that water, the pack lightens considerably.

OTHER STUFF Camera? I bring one almost every time, and rarely take a picture. On the rare occasion that I leave the camera behind, however, I always regret it. Super-fancy cameras should be stowed in a heavily padded something-or-other and placed in the core of the backpack, to protect against damage in the event of a head-over wreck. It's not unusual to flip over and land right on the backpack. I once broke a nice 35mm that way. (Film cameras—remember those?) Also, take care that your hydro-pack or bottles don't leak all over it.

Phone? I would say a phone could be useful in a worst-case scenario, but in such a worst-case scenario a phone wouldn't work anyway. But maybe you'll get lucky and the phone will be able to connect you to the civilized world after you or a friend is badly injured deep in the woods. A portable phone might be the only possible way to get a rescue started in a timely manner. It might even save somebody's life. With this thought in mind, I haul a cell phone along whenever I ride solo and like to have one or two along in a group. If one doesn't connect, maybe another will. Keep it turned off unless you need it; otherwise, it will be in a constant state of disconnecting and attempting to reconnect with the cell tower/satellite, and running its battery down in the process. (Also, it might ring while you're surfing some really sweet section, and you might pull over thinking *I'd better take that, it could be important,* and then find yourself standing trailside talking to some salesman or bill collector. That would be patently absurd.) If you need to call out and can't get service, try hiking to the top of the nearest hill.

Maybes: First-aid kit. Compass, weighs almost nothing, could be useful. Emergency blanket, small yet powerful. Pocketknife. Iodine pills. Extra socks. Moleskin (although a small adhesive bandage will do the trick). Bug dope—poison your skin so the skeeters won't eat it. Sunscreen. Lighter or dry matches. Votive candles.

THE GROUP Undeniably, it can turn into a bit of a competition. You measure yourself against your friends. Riding with the same people week after week, you become very well acquainted with their strengths and weaknesses on the bike. You can tell when they've improved, or when they're having a tough day. When you can keep up with or stay ahead of someone who's dropped immense tonnage of hurt onto you over the years, it feels good. But it can easily move beyond feeling good and into the realm of Payback Time.

The first two decades or so of mountain biking as a sport saw exaggerated expressions of mutual support among riders and racers—a lot of nice, helpful people patting each other on the back, and earnest fans offering encouragement from trailside. There was a sort of tribal sharing of the challenge and suffering involved, which at the time was still quite the novelty.

As that novelty wore off, so has the exaggerated intra-tribal goodwill. This laid bare something that was there the whole time, that element of sly rivalry and friendly competition. A degree of gamesmanship is bound to occur among a group of good friends who are not only comfortable with each other, but also quite close in ability. Somebody always says how slow and sick and weak they feel before the ride; once it starts, invariably, that person is off like a rabbit. I have one friend who is always standing around at the trailhead trying to scare the rest of us into carrying even more cold-weather gear and water than we already have—trying to trick us into hauling unnecessary weight in our packs relative to his. It took me a while to figure out what he was up to. We try to throw rocks surreptitiously into each other's packs during breaks in the ride.

Friends may know each other's weaknesses and attack them. One guy knows the other hasn't been able to ride a certain switchback: He might get off his bike and stand by the trail, offering "You got it!" to his friend and pointing out some good lines. He's probably more likely to stand on the pedals and take off. Even though there is no race today (officially), he's happy to abscond with that little advantage. Just to win the unspoken imaginary hill-climb points at the top. Just so everybody knows who is the strongest around these parts today, in case there was any confusion. Or maybe so he can get a little bit ahead for a moment and grab a rest.

This sounds like another stupid Man Thing, but beware of lazy thinking that blames the urge to crush one's riding mates on testosterone. The reality is that women also get into the act. There are plenty of female riders out there who are eager and able to put the screws to their "testosterone-fueled" counterparts, timing their efforts for maximum humiliation—it adds a whole 'nother level of fun for them, and is educational for the men too.

When the trail tips downward, the competition goes on—faster, and dangerous. The hot descender will try to make the little climber pay for indiscretions that occurred on the other side of the mountain. The lesser bike handler is pushed into situations beyond his ability, trying to keep up with, or trying to stay ahead of, a faster rider who is right on his wheel jabbering smack talk into his ear at 30 mph. He crashes, but he also improves. Later on everybody sits around and jokes about who was doing the punishing and who was getting punished, and just how and when all that was occurring. As long as nobody takes any of this too far, the group will be itching to get together again soon.

You don't have to keep the group in tight formation during the ride, but you do have to keep fairly close tabs on everybody. The slowest riders are likely to be found bringing up the rear, and they also tend to be the least skilled, and most likely to crash. This means that the caboose of the group could crash hard and that less-than-careful companions might not be able to find their friend and render aid or call for help for a very long time. Preventing such a disaster requires sacrifice. It means frequently stopping when you could be moving fast. It might mean turning around to check on someone who hasn't arrived in a few minutes. It might even mean riding at the back of the group at what seems like a snail's pace. Even with an experienced rider at the rear, of course, the group needs to confirm periodically that he or she is still back there and doing fine.

Critically, any time the lead rider arrives at a trail junction, he or she should stop and wait. Once the second rider arrives, the lead rider has a practical decision to make: continue to wait, or take off, delegating the second rider to wait? The second rider can wait for the third, the third can wait for the fourth, like that. Practically speaking, there is a good chance under the impatient accordion method that one or more will decide not to wait for the rider behind them—*ah, they know where to go*—and that someone will get a bit lost because of it. The sweeter the singletrack, the less anybody wants to interrupt the flow for slower riders.

The simple dynamic of faster riders waiting for slower ones at trail intersections can breed resentment within the group in sneaky ways. Significant hard feelings arise due to the simple reason that everybody tends to take off when the last rider arrives at the junction. If you're never the slow rider, maybe you've never really given it much thought. Everybody's hanging out, cracking jokes, drinking water, sharing energy bars and bananas—*resting*—then, as soon as that straggler arrives, the group saddles up and moves out. So the rider who probably needs to rest more than anyone else will feel, at best, rushed into continuing. Don't think they don't realize rather quickly how they're being screwed by their inconsiderate friends. They have a lot of time to think things over and boil with anger, as they straggle along behind the group by themselves. It's only fair to give the slowest riders some time to rest too, and wait with them while they relax and refuel.

The slow riders have special responsibilities in this scheme as well. Don't stress out about being the slow one, but don't make it any worse than it has to be. This may not be the best time, for instance, to set up the tripod and practice your wildflower macrophotography.

And let's not forget about the Arrow-Making People. It is quite common to come across arrows, made of twigs or rocks, lying in the dirt at trail junctions. These artifacts are evidence of a somewhat selfish and reckless civilization.

Arrow-making is a sign of mountain bikers who are too impatient to wait for those behind them. They run around gathering twigs and form them into an arrow flat on the ground. *This-a-way*. Usually this makeshift messaging works fine. But what if one of the slower or directionally challenged riders fails to notice the improvised sign, and rolls off into parts unknown? While engaged in riding singletrack, it is shockingly easy to roll past signs and intersections without noticing them. A makeshift signal on the ground could be overlooked very, very easily. More importantly, if the straggler has crashed, and is back there somewhere incapacitated, the arrow-makers won't figure this out.

Decency and caution demand that someone actually wait for the last rider to show up at the junction. If the caboose doesn't show within a reasonable time, retrace tracks and intercept, just to be sure everything's okay. It's important. He or she might be struggling with a flat tire or mechanical issue, or a broken bike or bone after a hard wreck.

If someone in the group does get separated, he may be able to reorient himself by tracking his riding partners. The group may be able to track down the lost lamb in the same way. At the trailhead, it doesn't hurt to take note of the types of tires and tread patterns of various members of the group. If one of the riders is using an unusual brand of tire, it can be quite easy to follow, even in popular trail networks. Obviously, if all the tread patterns are generic, the group's tracks can get lost among the rest. Tracking tire treads might seem a little nuts, but I've seen it come into play several times.

MISADVENTURE Adventurous riders embrace the dangers of biting off way more mountain biking than can be chewed in a single day. It's an interesting feeling to embark on a huge loop in the backcountry, get about halfway through, and realize, hey, it's going to get dark on my ass. Few carry lights that they don't plan on using; they're generally too heavy to be used as preventives. So you're out there in the dark, no lights. Maybe you can ride a little bit by moonlight, drunken monkey–style; maybe it's just too dark to ride at all. Hopefully you've got some warm clothes, food, water, a map. Getting lost or stuck doesn't have to be a big deal, if you've got the proper gear in the pack. One of those emergency blankets might come in handy, for instance; something to make a fire would be very nice in a worst-case scenario.

What's that? No gear whatsoever? Whoops. *You gonna die.* No, that's not true. Probably, you won't die (from that). But spending the night in the woods can be a pretty bad deal for someone who isn't prepared for it. I've never had to do that myself, although I've been very close a few times.

For several years it was the fashion among our group of messenger-mountain bikers to embark on trail rides that were very long and difficult—probably too long and difficult. If it didn't end in the dark, it wasn't a real ride. A lot of those epic adventures stand out in the memory. There was the long loop outside of Moab: Green River–Hey Joe Canyon–Dubinky Well. It's not so long, actually, maybe 35 miles, but it has this crazy cliff climb in the middle, sandpit roads at the end, and if you start the ride way too late like we did, you're screwed. That one involved a lot of huddling in the dark around a Bic lighter and a map, trying not to miss a crucial turn. Someone had to drive back out into the desert to pick up a poor chap named Kevin, a rider we had passed along the way who was having a very tough time. When Mike found Kevin he was in the somewhat desperate process of making his sand-bed next to the road in the howling wind.

Another ride out of Leadville ended near midnight and included the rescue of a kitten, neither of which was according to plan (long story). There was a lot of late-night rescuing going on in those days. Whether that is a good sign or a bad one, I'll leave it up to you to decide. If the one being rescued is you, it's probably not good.

A few years ago I was on a long solo ride in Colorado's Pike National Forest, and the sun had just gone down. Except for myself and some mule deer, the trails were deserted. Then, a little hole that had worn through one of the fingers of my glove got caught on the brake lever in such a way that I couldn't squeeze the lever right at a point where it was really, really important that I squeeze that sucker. In case you were wondering, that can happen. I crashed so hard into a downed tree next to the trail that I destroyed my frame and launched myself about 30 feet into the woods in a full back layout. Luckily, I wasn't badly injured, but I should have been. I really dodged a bullet with that one. I had to walk out many miles in the dark, trailing my broken machine, but I knew I was lucky.

While I was tuned in to the trail that day, I wasn't tuned in to the *situation*: riding alone, getting dark, with a very dangerous hole in my glove. Incidents like that highlight the importance of riding with other people, or at least around other people. Be especially careful in the late afternoon hours, when you might be the only human left for miles around. And make sure someone responsible knows where you're going, so when you don't come back, he or she can start freaking out. Do that person and your would-be rescuers a favor by adhering to the original plan. (And replace those gloves before any holes wear through the fingers.)

The most memorable of our epic rides occurred many years ago in Summit County, Colorado, and proved the importance of bringing extra gear and of having at least one accurate map, if not some foreknowledge of the route. Three friends and I were searching for a long, tough ride, preferably a loop we'd never ridden before, which was typical modus operandi for us and for lots of other cyclists. We found one on the map and went for it. Laughably, we wondered aloud at the trailhead if it would be enough, and were considering the possibility of doing it *twice*.

The trail we chose, not surprisingly for little-known routes, wasn't much of a trail at all, fading badly within 4 or 5 miles of the trailhead. But it periodically reemerged, luring us higher and higher up an endless valley. This was the type of riding we loved. So far, so good.

In the early afternoon we ate a long lunch, then decided that the loop was still within our grasp, even though we were still pretty far from the halfway point, with a huge climb ahead. All that afternoon we were on and off our bikes, trudging up a massive traverse; the tiny trail disintegrated into multiple rivulets then finally disappeared completely. Few people make it that far, apparently.

Someone suggested turning back. It was Rob. Should have listened to him. Instead, we called him names. We were into pushing our limits, so that's exactly what we did. We pushed on and on. Finally we made the top of the 12,000-foot ridge, the high point of the loop, at about five o'clock. We'd enjoyed about seven hours of climbing. All downhill from here, we thought. And the trail had even made something of a miraculous comeback, like Cher.

We ate the last of our food on the ridge, feeling tough, then picked our way down into the valley, back into the pines. Donald fell during the descent and dislocated a finger; popped it back into place. The trail disappeared, but we seemed to be on the right track nonetheless, so we kept on, bushwhacking around the trees.* About eight hours into the ride, the sun said good night and the air went cold. No problem, we thought, we can smell the trailhead from here, and we all have warm layers on board. It looked like we were going to get away with another one, finishing after dark.

At that point we came across a dirt road that didn't show on our map, but it seemed like it wanted to take us right down to the start/finish. Tricky. It was some kind of mining company service road, which, though several miles long and nicely maintained, formed a sort of horseshoe around the valley, with dead ends on both sides. But we didn't know that. It looked like a real road to us. We hit the dead end in complete darkness.

Rather than turn back, we decided our best bet would be to hike directly down to the valley floor where, according to the map, a trail would be waiting on the other side of a river. Trying to hike-a-bike down that heavily forested north-facing slope was an unbelievable task. In the daylight, with hiking boots and no bikes, it would have been ridiculous. The slope was extremely rocky, almost too steep to stand on, and there were hundreds, thousands, of huge snarling deadfalls that had to be scrambled over awkwardly with the bikes. It was a long way down, about 1,500 vertical feet. Amazingly, nobody snapped an ankle or poked an eye out. About

---

* In general, cyclists shouldn't ride off-trail. However, if you're off-trail anyway, riding with a soft style won't necessarily cause more damage than walking, or walking with a bike.

halfway down, one of the trees ripped the valve stem off my front wheel and laughed maniacally.

We arrived at the bottom after an hour or two of struggle, our shins streaked with blood, and immediately started slogging through waste-deep water—because there was no easy way around it, and we figured the trail would be right there on the other side, as our map indicated. But the trail wasn't there, or at least we couldn't find it in the dark. The forest was so thick, we ended up pushing our bikes straight down the river in the general direction of the trailhead for more than a mile. And then, what's this? A crude bridge lay across the water. The damn trail! We happened across it in our infinite luck. It was too dark then to ride at all (no moon whatsoever), and even if it hadn't been, my bike wasn't exactly functional at that point. But we were happy to have located a real trail nonetheless.

However, the mountain wasn't content to let us off the hook just yet. At some point, we lost the trail *again,* and wandered around for another surreal hour searching for it. Failing to locate an escape route, we felt resigned to the night. It had been many hours since any of us had eaten a bite of food. We were cold, wet, bloody, and exhausted. By then we had been out for over fourteen hours. I remember sitting on the ground against a log and falling into involuntary sleep. I wouldn't say our lives were in jeopardy, but it was kind of a serious situation. A while later I heard Steve F. call out, "I found it!" He had never stopped searching for the trail. Thanks to him we got back to our warm beds that night, about 3:00 a.m.

It was a hell of a "ride," and I'll never forget it.

BASIC TRAIL ETIQUETTE Trail etiquette is pretty simple.

- Bicyclists give way to hikers.

- Bicyclists and hikers give way to horses. (When encountering horses, dismount and move yourself and your bike well off the trail, out of kicking range. Some horses are freaked by the machinery, how it looks and sounds. Calmly greet the riders so the animals know they're dealing with another human instead of some new type of alien life-form.)

- When encountering another cyclist on the trail, the downhill rider
  gives way to the uphill rider. (Downhill riders yielding to climbers
  should stop, move their bikes to the edge of the trail, and lean
  away from it with one foot down, rather than riding off-trail and
  trampling the vegetation.) Riders should also disclose if they are
  being followed by others.

Despite the simplicity of these rules, they are often forgotten,
neglected, or selectively ignored. For example, it often happens that a
hiker or group of hikers will step off the trail to let a mountain biker go
by. In fact, this may happen more often than not when hikers and bikers
come together. It's almost automatic. The hikers tend to have at least a
vague understanding of their right-of-way, but it just seems easier to them
in that moment to step off the trail. Trail riders can take advantage of this
abdication of right-of-way seamlessly, either with a gracious greeting that
acknowledges the hikers' going above and beyond the call of duty, or with
a stone-faced blur of a snub that makes the hikers want to go home and
write nasty Internet comments about selfish mountain bikers all night
long. Cyclists, on both road and trail, need to apply more finesse to their
brief social interactions.

Sometimes there will be enough room for two cyclists on a trail to get
past each other without stopping. That works as long as both riders have
similar ideas about how much room is enough; otherwise, somebody's
feelings get hurt.

Another common scenario—a rider descending a singletrack with
too much gusto comes around a curve and encounters an uphill rider.
There comes a sudden realization that there isn't enough time/space for
the downhiller to yield. Obviously the downhiller's mistake can result in
a collision, but most often the errant rider will simply end up rolling or
bouncing past, or skidding to an awkward stop near the climber. A clear
violation of the time-honored rules, yes, but not a sign that the end is nigh.
The correct sequence of events in response to such a common occurrence should perhaps be incorporated into the trail etiquette booklets and
signage: The careening downhiller apologizes, profusely, and the climber

accepts the apology, and everybody keeps going. Hopefully the descender will resume with toned-down gusto and under control, more mindful of the likelihood of encountering other trail users. Sometimes the aggrieved climber wants to make a federal case out of it, which isn't helpful.

In addition to the basic rules about interacting with other trail users, there are traditional rules about how to treat trails, the woods, and wildlife: Try not to skid, or ride off-trail or on muddy trails; don't trample around too much or leave anything behind; and don't spook the animals. Another set of deceptively simple don't-do's, most of which occur as a normal part of mountain biking.

PART III

THE BIG PICTURE

TOO MANY I lost count after fifteen or so. One kid after another came down the trail at me in a cloud of red dust and a hail of feldspar pebbles. Unlike some of the adults I met on the trail that day, who apparently didn't get the memo on basic trail etiquette, almost all the kids took pains to stop and move their bikes from the singletrack to let me climb past. They seemed to be middle-school-aged kids, maybe thirteen or fourteen, and so carefully drilled in old-school mountain bike mores, they must have been part of an established club. In sharp contrast to the clunky, oversize trail bikes that were available when I was their age, most of these kids rode fancy, light full-suspension bikes. (When I was their age, mountain biking itself was still in diapers; see page xi.)

The parade of kid trail jockeys sparked some conflicting emotions. It was heartwarming to see all these kids out having fun in the woods. A rare sight these days. American kids' participation in all outdoor activities has been on a downhill slope.[1] These kids were way ahead of their couch-locked peers. On the other hand, the sheer numbers were ominous. It was, as one of my riding buddies said, "pretty [f-ing] cool." And, as another who was there that day said, "kind of like queuing up for toilet paper in the USSR."

These historically lonely trails had been getting noticeably busier all season, then, just before the first decisive snowfall—long after the point when the dabblers should have been tucked into their Snugglies watching the final, climactic episodes of *El Clon*—more clogged than ever before. The situation didn't bode well for the following summer. Having retreated to these trails for over twenty years, seeking relief from human contact, among other things, I felt a light buzz of dread rise in my belly. That solitude appeared to be in serious jeopardy. The area* seemed to have entered the exponential straight-up rocket launch phase of its popularity curve.

I imagined all these mountain biking kids going back to wherever they were from and telling all their friends how great these trails are. That's

---

* We say that a certain "area" is popular. That's fine for activities like hunting or skiing where participants range throughout a large zone, but in mountain biking all the action occurs on the thin strip of real estate known as the trail, so the size of the area is irrelevant. What matters is how much trail is available.

how it works. And then all of those kids spawn 2.3 more kids, all infected with the mountain bike gene, all flocking to the same trails. The numbers, the numbers. Numbers can crush the future of mountain biking.

For decades the dominant inclination, either natural or unnatural, has been to *sell* the fledgling sport and keep participation growing. This growth comes with several negative consequences for the actual trail rider. The density of users (humans-per-foot of singletrack) compromises the rider's ability to commune with nature in peace—to achieve that Into the Wild feeling of being small and alone in the woods. The frequency of passing also destroys the flow that mountain bikers crave. This is especially true for downhill riders encountering large groups climbing toward them. Instead of having to pull over every few seconds, which will ruin the descent, it's better to wait at the top for the whole crew to pass, then resume.

Trail overpopulation also adds a certain amount of danger to the whole enterprise, even for the cyclist creeping slowly uphill. What is normally a distant, faint consideration becomes an ever-present worry: Around any blind corner could be a hurtling nincompoop like myself. This represents outright defeat for the trail rider's sense of freedom from the danger of traffic (see page 75). So right away we see that the presence of so many other people has sabotaged three of our favorite things about the sport.

Successful trail riding depends on lots of free space and lots of open trail, however discomforting that reality may be. If a critical mass of riders attempts to enjoy the same trail on the same day, it will ruin the ride for all of them.

Of course, it is good for a few laughs to watch profligate trail-cloggers like myself complaining about overuse of singletrack. I hear you laughing out there. I know I don't have a leg to stand on. The fact that I've written guidebooks encouraging people to get out and ride adds bonus absurdity.

It seems we're going to need more trails or fewer mountain bikers. One potential solution that has been tossed around lately, and which makes a lot of sense to me, is to invade a small country in South America, or a particularly scenic portion of Canada, and annex their trails. Alternatively, different forms of restricted access will need to be instituted at problem areas to arrest any Tragedy-of-the-Commons downward spirals. We have only ourselves to blame.

IMPACT The serenity felt by the mountain biker, or hiker, communing with nature in the woods, is really an illusion. In the surrounding forest, waves of alarm reverberate outward from the human's position. Animals of all sizes are in full flight, slinking away or paralyzed in fear. Black squirrels scramble into the crowns of Douglas fir and cackle warnings to their families. Chipmunks and voles lose their minds and dart back and forth to thwart an impending air attack. A group of mule deer crashes through a spiky deadfall and into a rock canyon, leaving two fawns behind. Turmoil—caused only by your presence.

You'll have to excuse these animals. After tens of thousands of years of evolutionary hard-wiring, they simply assume you're there to kill anything that moves.

Hikers and horsemen like to think they're more in harmony with the natural world than the relative newcomers rolling through on flashy equipment and wearing shiny gear. Even I would have bought that one for a dollar, but it doesn't appear to be the case. Plenty of evidence shows that animals will display much more ambivalence toward a vehicle than a human on foot, who they identify immediately as a primal threat, even if it happens to be wearing natural fibers and smells like earth. A mountain biker, moving quickly and often quietly, is unlikely to cause more alarm than a hiker.[2] On the other hand, mountain bikers can cover a lot more distance, and thus may impact greater numbers of animals.

Unfortunately, the impact inflicted on wildlife by the trail rider can be a literal, deadly impact. If you think about it, it's one of the weirdest ways a forest creature could possibly die. Incidents are rare, but not rare enough. Usually it's one of the aforementioned darting rodents, darting right under a knobby tire as it rolls by. Sometimes a snake. Every once in a while you see one of the poor mangled victims trailside, sacrificed to outdoor recreation.

Keep these little creatures in your thoughts as you ride, and be ready to twist or hop your front or back tire around their darting forms if one pops out from the edge like a toddler chasing a ball into the street. For that matter, think of the beetles, the spiders, the ants, and the other bugs which are part of a healthy ecosystem. If you can see them on the trail, you can avoid them. Maneuvering around these insects is good practice for learning to control both lines. For extra credit, take a moment to move any large, slow-moving insects out of harm's way.

Of course, the very act of riding a bike on the trail will, unavoidably, cause the demise of great numbers of tiny creatures, such as mites feeding on organic material in the soil, and other members of the "soil population." So will hiking, with collateral damage under every step. So will sitting in a chair, or touching your eyelashes.

TRAILISM *Don't skid on the trails! Don't ride on wet or muddy trails! Ee-aarrggh!*

People get real emotional and squeal like Howard Dean about erosion damage to trails caused by skidding mountain bike tires, or unnecessary widening of trails caused by mountain bikers riding around muddy spots. But we tend to forget all about the damage to the *ecosystem* caused by the trail's very existence. That fits the pattern these days: Ignore the big picture, which makes us look bad and which we lack any real guts to change; focus on the itty-bitty inconsequential issues that allow us to feel self-righteous and in control. Defending trail surfaces on environmental grounds is kind of like driving a hybrid Tahoe.

It makes sense to design and create sustainable trails, and to work to preserve them in their pristine skinniness and urge fellow users to do the same. It is absurd to put on an air of self-righteousness for this work of preserving trails or to confuse it with any sort of higher environmental calling—because trails themselves are bad for the environment. A popular singletrack is going to cause significant problems for the ecosystem it dissects, on several levels.

Starting from the bottom of the food chain: Particularly in delicate alpine and arid ecosystems, the trail represents a loss of the highly adapted groundcover that is critical for sustaining all life forms in the immediate vicinity; it takes forever to grow, a few seconds to destroy, and forever to grow back. It's nice to keep people rolling or walking on the already worn-in trail, instead of trampling subalpine shrubs which spend a month or two slowly dying after a single encounter with a lugged sole or bicycle tire, but keeping people on the trail is hardly an ecosystem-saving strategy.

Some birds will disrupt preferred migration and nesting patterns to avoid the trail corridor, or more precisely, the people on it. Large animals like elk will reduce their normal range and huddle on steep hillsides to keep a safe distance from the trail and its unwelcome inhabitants.[3] Keeping the trail's surface baby smooth won't do the disturbed wildlife a bit of good. In fact, let's just admit we would have more positive environmental impact if we would stop preserving trails and start messing them up. The animals would thank us for making popular groomed trails more difficult to ride, or removing them altogether.*

Trail preservation can hardly be called a pure environmentalist goal, but shouldn't it be a mountain biking goal? Sure, to an extent. It's fun to ride smooth, undamaged trails. Keeping skinny trails skinny and fast trails fast is a righteous thing. But if we see some ruts or other funkiness along the way—and surely we will, no matter what kind of trail preservation efforts are in effect—we'll figure that out too. (Ruts are just tiny berms anyway.) The kind of mountain biking we're talking about here is about dealing with a constant stream of varied challenges, whatever the trail throws down, and isn't dependent on groomed, prepared surfaces.

Bottom line: It's just a trail. Don't get all sentimental about it.

THE DESIGN AND DESTRUCTION OF AMERICAN TRAILS For those concerned with trail surfaces, it's now well understood that the best way to keep a singletrack trail in good shape is to design it right in the first place. Primarily this means routing to avoid prolonged steep slopes, thus

---

* A counterargument has been offered in favor of trails: Preserving trail surfaces promotes outdoor recreation, brings more people into the natural areas, and thereby fosters greater appreciation for environmental concerns over the long term.

creating longer, somewhat more meandering trails. What determines if a trail is too steep? It depends on the composition of the trail surface and the physical geography of the immediate vicinity. This can vary a lot along the same trail (as it switches from one side of the mountain to the other, for instance). On a too-steep section, the normal movements of hikers, animals, and bicyclists are distorted into friction-seeking lurches that systematically destroy the trail surface—skidding and grinding.

> " This trail owns me.
> —**Unidentified party, standing next to Forest Service Trail 409, 2009**

Flatten the trail out, lengthen it, and nobody needs to skid and grind. During rainstorms that would have little transformative effect on a good trail, the too-steep trail becomes a channel for the water, and any nascent ruts are opened wide.*

The trail designer's primary task is to account for inevitable flare-ups of the forces in nature associated with severe weather. A poorly designed trail will be rutted out within a single season, even if nobody uses it. A well-designed trail will endure for *generations* and will provide a much more enjoyable riding experience—unless it attracts so many users all at once that it clogs harder than the arteries of a trucker eating a sloppy joe at a diner in Tulsa. Even then, everyone will see that the trail itself remains substantially in its original condition, the way well-designed trails do.

On multiuser-used singletrack the destructive power of mountain biking relative to other types of use is overstated and overhyped. There is no doubt that mountain bikers carve ruts and "braking bumps" into trails with their skidding and sliding. The more riders there are, the worse it is. As with the impact on wildlife, however, mountain bikers are not especially destructive compared to hikers. Studies show that the constant,

---

* Trail designer Randy Martin writes: "What is called the half rule applies to specific grade: The slope of the trail should not be more than one half the cross slope. . . . The reason for this rule is that if the trail is too steep, relative to the slope of the hill, water will tend to collect and run down the trail instead of sheet flowing across the trail and down the hill. Keep in mind that every turn violates this rule at one point. Grade reversals (dips), if used generously, force the water off the trail and can counter violations of this rule."[4]

percussive heel-toe grind of the hiking boot causes damage to vegetation and trail surfaces that is comparable to or worse than the damage caused by knobby bike tires. Horses and motorcycles are on another plane in terms of destructive potential.[5]

STREAM CROSSINGS
Almost by definition, stream crossings occur at the low point of a section of singletrack. Often there's a quick, fast downhill, transitioning within a few feet to a steep climb, and the short transition zone is underwater. It's difficult to "ride light" through such a short transition, as the bike is shoved into the ground with g-forces. For this reason and others, stream crossings tend to involve a lot of crashing and bashing, blind grip-the-bars-and-go-for-it-style riding. This leads to comical dunkings of hapless riders. Good times.

Less hilariously, every attempt, successful or comical, results in significant damage to the stream's microenvironment as tires churn up material from the bottom and cloud the water. This disturbance increases sediment concentration in the stream, usually at a relatively high point in the stream biome, which has adapted to low levels of suspended sediment and higher levels of oxygen. In other words, stirring up big clouds of sediment seriously messes with the flora and fauna of a mountain stream.[6] Every stream crossing is an unnatural disaster.

There's an easy solution for this: Stop trying to ride through streams. Instead, pick up the bike and jump across, if possible, or carefully step on fixed rocks or logs to get to the other side (crashing through the stream on foot won't do it any good).

The stream crossing has been a loveable, stand-out feature of our trail rides for the past several decades. We need to get over it, literally and figuratively. The streams are too important to be thrashed for our amusement. New trails should be equipped with bridges, or at least stepping stones. Existing trails can be retrofitted with these at crossings or, if the stream in question isn't very wide, *ramps* on either side. Don't ride through streams—jump over them. Do the forest a huge favor by keeping its water-bearing arteries clean.

MECHANICAL TRANSPORT By the late nineteenth century, the railroads had been laid across the mountains and through them. The Mountain Utes, whose previous domain had included a huge portion of the Rocky Mountains, were removed at gunpoint to the desert, making way for the thorough aeration of the Rockies by the burgeoning mineral-extraction industry; in the process of booming-and-busting itself a few times before the turn of the century, the industry pushed its pack trails and wagon roads up every drainage between Denver and San Francisco. In the meantime, hunters harvested wild beasts like elk and grizzlies from the forests in huge numbers, measuring their success by the wagonload.

Out on the Great Plains, the bison were long gone, and the trouble-some tribes like the Cheyenne and Arapahoe had been decimated decades earlier. Millions of cattle spilled into the void, systematically chewing and stomping anything not already fenced off by settlers. It was quite a deal for anybody enterprising enough to raise, move, and sell herds of cattle, to have the entire midriff of the country, from Texas to Chicago, at your disposal for free. All of this changed the American wilderness swiftly and inexorably—the *wild* was hunted, trapped, mined, grazed, logged, and genocided right out of it (not necessarily in that order).

At this point there came a widespread realization that government should get involved with conserving wild areas, or at least rationing out the remaining bits of them for various industrial uses, before they were all gobbled up. This is known as closing the barn door through which the horses have already skittered. The first formal step in the creation of the managed terrarium-like situation that we enjoy today was the National Forest Reserves Act of 1891.

Today, most of the emblematic American mountain bike trails are in the national forests. In fact, almost all the mountain bike trail riding that occurs in the United States happens on some form of public land, whether national forest, Bureau of Land Management land, or state or locally owned parcels set aside as "open space" or parks. Mountain biking as we know and understand it here depends on public land. And lots of it. Yet there are vast swaths of the public American landscape from which mountain bikers are barred from entering, at least with our bicycles.

In 1964, in another rare spasm of conservation-minded activity, the U.S. Congress passed the Wilderness Act. The act decreed that certain areas of existing national forests, relatively "untrammeled by man, where man himself is a visitor who does not remain," would be set aside and allowed to age naturally in their "primeval character" for the foreseeable future.

One particular section of the Wilderness Act concerns us here:

> *Except as specifically provided for in this chapter, and subject to existing private rights, there shall be no commercial enterprise and no permanent road within any wilderness area designated by this chapter and, except as necessary to meet minimum requirements for the administration of the area for the purpose of this chapter (including measures required in emergencies involving the health and safety of persons within the area), there shall be no temporary road, no use of motor vehicles, motorized equipment or motorboats, no landing of aircraft,* no other form of mechanical transport, *and no structure or installation within any such area.*[7]

It's unlikely that the authors of the above passage, in 1964, even considered the possibility of lunatic hippies riding modified bicycles on mountain trails. It would have been easy to clarify the language of the law in favor of bicycles, once the abstract thought popped into someone's head, by excluding *human-powered* devices from the "mechanical transport" subset. A 1966 Forest Service ruling did just that, strangely enough, stating that only machines "propelled by a non-living power source" would be prohibited. But things turned around immediately when the mountain bike idea was actualized.

Long before the sport escaped the '70s, the Forest Service was preparing to banish bicycles from wilderness areas. By 1984, not long after the Stumpjumper had flashed into the mainstream consciousness, the agency ruled conclusively that mountain bikes were indeed "mechanical transport" and would be banned. Finally, the 1990 *Forest Service Manual* gave the new definition of "mechanical transport," specially crafted to exclude bicycles from wilderness areas: ". . . any contrivance for moving people or material in or over land, water, or air, having moving parts, that provides a mechanical advantage to the user, and that is *powered by a living or nonliving power source*. This includes, but is not limited to, sailboats, hang gliders, parachutes, bicycles, game carriers, carts, and wagons."[8] And so it was.

In the past half-century, the number and total acreage of designated wilderness areas has skyrocketed. Originally there were fifty-four; in 2010 there were roughly eight hundred. As more land is designated, mountain bikers find themselves banned from increasing numbers of trails that had already become old favorites. This puts us in a very tough spot. Many mountain bikers are self-described environmentalists and conservationists who like the general concept behind the Wilderness Act, wildlife protection zones, things like that. More often than not, we'll express a willingness to help preserve these parcels in a relatively undisturbed condition. Even if the ban on bicycles runs counter to the intent of the original law, bicyclists have never been all that fired up about overturning the exclusion. In fact, they're more or less on board with it. But nobody likes to be unfairly singled out. What rankles is the inconsistency and apparent selectivity of the rule.

As we've seen already, the environmental disturbance created by a human on a bicycle is not greater than the disturbance caused by someone on foot or horseback (see page 102). While disallowing individual cyclists, the Forest Service seems to have little problem with sizable parties entering wilderness areas on horses and packing in massive amounts of gear to set up semipermanent hunting camps so they can really go to town on the local animal population. It's hard to see how one activity goes against the spirit of the Wilderness Act while the other does not.

Furthermore, as Theodore Stroll pointed out in a 2004 paper in the *Penn State Environmental Law Review,* the ban on "mechanical transport," if taken at face value, would snare all kinds of devices that are commonly used in wilderness areas, including "alpine and mountaineering skis, rowboats with oarlocks, antishock hiking poles, and climbing gear."[9]

For the greater good, mountain bikers have nobly resisted heaping piles of ridicule and vitriol on the regulators who continue to punish them with this tortured interpretation of the law.

Rather than simply lashing out when any new wilderness designation is proposed, the International Mountain Bike Association (IMBA) has adopted a nuanced approach to the issue, supporting the creation of new wilderness areas, while working with the authorities to preserve access for mountain bikers on a trail-by-trail basis, through the use of boundary adjustments and special corridors. The art of compromise. Soft power, people. Their enlightened strategy has been somewhat effective in keeping important trails open and even opening new ones, while some others go off-limits.

IMBA thinks that mountain biking can grow as a sport and still be sustainable, environmentally and otherwise. I really hope they're right.

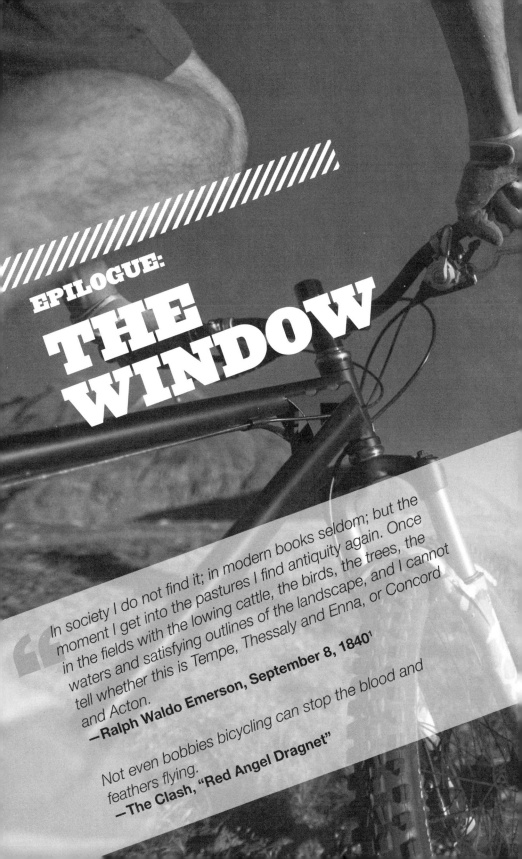

EPILOGUE:
THE WINDOW

In society I do not find it; in modern books seldom; but the moment I get into the pastures I find antiquity again. Once in the fields with the lowing cattle, the birds, the trees, the waters and satisfying outlines of the landscape, and I cannot tell whether this is Tempe, Thessaly and Enna, or Concord and Acton.
—**Ralph Waldo Emerson, September 8, 1840**[1]

Not even bobbies bicycling can stop the blood and feathers flying.
—**The Clash, "Red Angel Dragnet"**

Lee McCormack, in his book *Mastering Mountain Bike Skills* (an excellent resource, by the way), claims that the sensation of speed is the main factor that draws folks to the sport of mountain biking[2]. For many of us, especially the downhillers and other gravity-drunk freaks, that may very well be true. Speeding through the woods is incredible.

Old-school Moab guide Lee Bridgers has a different take: "The single most important draw of riding a mountain bike is NATURE."[3] True, there's a lot of that going on as well. Can't beat hanging out in the great outdoors, smelling the trees.

To some, the supreme workout that trail riding gives is probably the primary attraction. For others, it's the technical challenge, impossible to master even after decades of experience, that keeps them coming back for more. And we discussed the attraction of a riding venue free of cars and trucks.

Obviously, mountain biking represents many different things to many different people. But simply saying that mountain bike trail riding is so cool because it combines the sensation of speed, exercise, and technical challenge with the experience of nature—even that doesn't begin to do it justice. Mountain biking is much bigger than the sum of all these parts.

Mountain biking changed my whole relationship to the world, my perception of it, my enjoyment of it, my attitude in life, my perception of myself, the function of my vital organ systems, and my physical shape. Mountain biking completely and utterly rearranged my priorities. It connected me not just to nature, but to some mystical realm that I won't claim to understand. Sometimes when I'm out in the woods on the bike, I feel like I can commune with the dead. I can see 10,000 years into the past and breathe Anasazi air. I talk to my grandmothers.

Almost every time I ride my mountain bike in the woods, I am overwhelmed by feelings of thankfulness and joy. It is indeed a spiritual experience. The whole situation seems impossible.

What did I do to deserve this? Nothing, I think, other than practice enough to perform the activity. It's pure luck, to happen to live within a certain window of history—the Mountain Bike Epoch.

Having studied the history of these mountains, I can't help but think about the way things used to be around here. For generations, Ute and

Cheyenne-Arapahoe warriors, hungry for enemy horses and the special respect reserved for those who display bravery in combat, engaged in brutal intertribal skirmishes that often ended in hand-to-hand fights to the death, and the taking of scalps. These pine-covered foothills along the Front Range served as a natural buffer zone between the warring tribes—Utes in the mountains and Cheyenne-Arapahoe on the plains. War parties from both groups swept through the area to perform their raids, but the jagged strip of land along the mountains was regarded by everyone as too dangerous to linger in for long, and the roaming villages stayed well away from it.

As a Cheyenne or Ute Indian, it would have been difficult to sit and relax by a nice fat ponderosa pine as I'm doing now, feet dug into the crunchy feldspar gravel. Every sound the forest could produce, every sparrow in the brush, every skittering chipmunk, would become a warrior from the wrong tribe loading a bow or creeping up to take your scalp. Under those circumstances, I imagine one's inclination would be to keep moving, very quietly and deliberately, with a weapon in hand.

Whites had been living on the Front Range for a long time, trading and intermarrying with the Indians. Starting in 1858, a human wave of emigrants from the States swept into the area. Most were looking to get rich quick. The unimaginative leaders of the invaders soon arrived at a kill-'em-all strategy toward the Indians, and the level of violence and evil on the Front Range ticked sharply upward. Massacres—that's how the West was won.

When the War of the Rebellion (aka the Civil War) broke out at about the same time, these foothills became contested ground in that conflict as well. The fledgling Colorado Territory raised a regiment of volunteers from the goldfields and settlers' sons and marched them south to battle the Texas Rangers near what is now the prime mountain biking area of northern New Mexico.

In these forests men hunted—creeping around with bows and arrows and rifles—not only beasts but other men. But right now, for the time being, no opposing factions are trying to kill each other around here. It's really quite amazing, a historical anomaly. So I sit today, on a rotting old tree trunk deep in these same old contested woods, just listening, with virtually no thoughts devoted to the possibility of getting shanked by an enemy, or eaten by a large animal. My most immediate concerns include a distant thunderstorm and the possibility that some sort of chigger may run up my shorts. Times sure have changed.

At some point, this window of recreational opportunity will surely slam shut. Judging by how things are going, it seems possible that we might be heading back toward that dark conception of the American woods—a place that you might enter alone and reasonably expect not to come back out. As they say, things fall apart. This would really mess with our mountain biking. If I'm lucky, we won't get there in my lifetime.

Been trail riding for more than a few decades now. It's gone by in a blur. The speed of time is breathtaking, isn't it? I swear the earth has been speeding up in its rotation and orbit. The question I ask myself more and more is, how many more trail rides can I get in, you know, before the curtain falls? Eventually that window of opportunity slips shut on every one of us. In the meantime, each ride is precious.

APPENDIX A: BUYING A MOUNTAIN BIKE

It's by far the most frequently asked question in mountain biking: *Which bike should I get?* This question has threatened to suck all the life out of the sport, and it'll suck the life out of this book if we're not careful. I'd prefer to pretend it doesn't exist. Unfortunately, it must be addressed.

Before you can answer the question, you have to know what kind of riding you want to do with this hypothetical bicycle, because the term "mountain biking" is used in reference to a variety of activities that are really quite different. These types of riding are so different that they require fundamentally different types of equipment.

In the past decade a lot of attention has been given to a certain type of riding called "freeride," which involves jumping, launching, rolling, and free-falling down extreme terrain. Sometimes freeriders find their own routes, and sometimes they go to a dedicated "freeride park" with lots of man-made jumps, gaps, and alligator pits. Freeriders push the limits of what is physically possible on a bicycle with the *current* laws of physics, and the video camera is often rolling. The discipline is related to old-school "downhill," in which bikes and riders are shuttled to the top of the hill and bomb down, but downhillers tend to stay on a trail and race against the clock, whereas freeriders go for magnitude and style, and whatever the heck they feel like. It's typical for this gravity-dependent joyriding to occur at a ski resort in the summer.

So the first question you need to ask is: Are you one of these downhillers or freeriders? A crazy headlong leaper? Launching yourself off cliffs and down avalanche chutes, sailing through the air in a majestic parabolic flight-path? If you are, you'd probably know it already. But it's possible that you aspire to live the life of a projectile in the future. Then we've certainly got a bike for you. You can choose from several different subtypes, in fact, that are all built on the same theme, jumps and drops. This equipment is necessarily very, very strong and relatively heavy; frame angles are more laid back. If you don't plan on climbing anything, why not? Even if you possessed the skill to perform extreme freeride maneuvers on a cross-country bike, doing so could break the frame or some other critical component, with potentially disastrous results.

I have a lot of respect for the skills of the great freeriders and downhillers, but they still represent a relatively small sect among off-roaders. If you're going to be riding like the vast majority of mountain bikers, you'll spend almost all of your time with wheels on the ground. The impacts that you and your bike are likely to receive will be far less extreme than those depicted in the freeride videos. You won't be screaming down the side of a mountain, as you may be imagining, but rolling uphill as well as down on widely varied terrain, often at very low speed. In fact, most of your time spent riding a typical trail will be spent pointed noticeably uphill, unromantic as that may seem. That's just an undeniable fact of life with trail riding, and a critically important one.*

Much of mountain bike marketing in the past decade is a push to convince ordinary trail riders that they should be using beefy long-travel bikes, derived from freeride bikes. Who can blame them? Gotta sell, sell, sell, and that's quite an angle. Manufacturing new must-have categories is how the bike companies get old mountain bikers to buy new bikes. Eventually they will come around to selling them the same bikes they had twenty years ago, you see. Meanwhile, the demands of normal singletrack riding (aka cross-country) are the same today as they were in 1982, 1992, or 2002. For this type of riding, a so-called cross-country bike will provide

---

* This is true for any cross-country trail ride that begins and ends at the same point, as long as the rider is slower climbing than descending. Point-to-point rides may have significantly more descending than climbing.

more than adequate beef and suspension. If it feels like you need more, it's very likely because something is lacking with the rider, not the bike.

Beware of claims about bikes that are some combination of freeride and cross-country and supposedly "bridge the gap" between them, allowing the rider to purchase a single bike that "does it all." It's not a gap that should be bridged in the first place. Should we bridge the gap between dinner and dessert, mix in a little meat loaf with our strawberry pie so we can enjoy them both at the same time? How would that taste? Best of both worlds, right?

Authors of mountain bike books are apparently supposed to list and extol the virtues of all the various new subgenres of mountain bike that have been birthed in the last decade: "Enduro," "All-Mountain," "Trail," etc.—all variations on the idea of bringing longer travel and slack angles to the trail. Well, you won't hear it from me. The attributes that make a bicycle shine on rough descents and large drops will make it behave like a stubborn pig on the climbs. With a bike, you really *can't* have it both ways. You *can't* have the best of both worlds. You can have the best of one or the other, a compromise somewhere in between, or, if you're not careful, the worst of both.

In short, if you're looking to acquire a bike, get a tool that is appropriate for the job. That means, for most of you, a so-called cross-country bike. For a relatively small number of you, who want to put all your eggs in the descending basket, it means a bike built for luging and launching. For an even smaller number, it means one of each: If you want to engage in completely different types of off-road riding, it's advisable to get completely different types of bikes. That's my opinion.

Cross-country trail bikes have evolved over the decades, in a complex response to demand, suggestion, and overall culture, so that now a wide variety exists even within this genre. Now you can get a cross-country rig in one of three basic varieties: front suspension/hardtail, full-suspension, or, very rarely anymore, full rigid. Each type has advantages and disadvantages, but any cross-country bike thoughtfully designed for climbs as well as descents will do, tweaked for personal preferences. Just make sure it fits well (see page 19).

It will be difficult to find a rigid trail bike with gears on it new in a shop (most of the new rigid bikes are single speeds). However, the old rigid bikes are such orphans that you might be able to pick up a high-quality '90s machine for *free* just by asking around among friends and coworkers. If you can snake something like an early '90s Stumpjumper or Bridgestone MB-2, your fun-to-expense ratio just went to infinity.

APPENDIX B: TWO-NINE

I am faced with the unfortunate necessity of pointing out that mountain bikes are now offered in a few different wheel sizes. Traditionally, mountain bike rims are "26-inch." Around the turn of this century, the bike biz rolled out the "29-inch" sizing for off-road bikes. Upping the wheel diameter has some interesting effects on a bike's handling characteristics, lengthening and narrowing the contact patch between tire and trail, stretching the wheelbase a bit, messing around with gyroscopic forces and the center of gravity in mysterious ways.

As with any modifications perpetrated on a bicycle, there will be trade-offs. Mountain bikers are currently engaged in arguing about the exact nature of the alleged benefits and drawbacks. Here's the *Cliff's Notes* version: The bigger wheels roll over obstacles easier and are more stable, at the expense of weight and maneuverability. It's easier to accelerate and turn the smaller wheel; the larger wheel holds its momentum better and provides more traction. Quite a few riders claim to prefer the "two-niner's" funky characteristics, however ill-defined, over the traditional setup.

Ye ol' curmudgeons like to point out that the two-niner was not an answer to some deficiency in traditional mountain bikes, but began as another marketing ploy from an industry desperate to hold the consumer's attention. Almost no mountain bikers were demanding larger wheels, or expressing any sort of need for them. There was no groundswell of demand for these things. People have become convinced, however, to jump on the two-nine bandwagon, and once they're up there, they always try to recruit their riding buddies, a self-reinforcing marketing circle.

It's important to realize that the two-nine wheel size isn't some new development, as the marketers would have you believe. It's just a wide tire on a 700c-size wheel—a traditional-size wheel.* Curmudgeonly speaking, it's basically a road wheel that they stuck on a mountain bike. How convenient that is for the rim manufacturers. Just use the same machines to make

---

* This gets confusing. A "29-inch" mountain bike uses rims the same diameter as traditional road rims: 622 millimeters, which is about 24.5 inches. However, the diameter of the wheel as a whole includes the tire as well. The terms "two-nine," "26-inch," and "700c" refer to the approximate diameter of a wheel including tires. A traditional "26-inch" mountain bike rim has a bead-to-bead diameter of 559 millimeters. "700c" and "29-inch" wheels are known as "28-inch" in Europe.

slightly wider hoops, put different stickers on them, and call it a sensation. Make that . . . a "revolution." Making suspension forks widely available for the larger wheel size opened the door to its commercial success.

A lot of top riders disagree with the above negative-tinged assessment. Jeremy Horgan-Kobelski, for instance, thinks the two-niner gives him a "huge advantage."[1] JHK's a pretty tall guy though.

Intrigued by the two-nine concept, I've often thought that something around a "27-inch" wheel would be just about right for my size and style of trail riding. A few manufacturers are now making "650b" (584 millimeters bead-to-bead) mountain bikes, very close to that in-between wheel size I've been considering. That could be just what the doctor ordered. It's still too early to see how all this shakes out.

That's already way too much discussion about equipment. Get a bike. Learn to ride it.

APPENDIX C: GLOSSARY

auger: To crash due to a sudden twisting of the front wheel, which plows into the dirt. Any kind of plow-like action of the front wheel.

babyhead: A loose rock roughly the size of a baby's head, known to cause technical issues for off-road cyclists. Often found gathered with other babyheads in large collections.

berm: A smooth banked outside edge of a curved section of trail, usually man-made. Like the banking of a NASCAR track, smooth berms allow riders to "rail" turns without slowing down.

biff: (*v.*) Crash.

bonk: To completely run out of gas, due to exhaustion and/or failure to eat properly.

bottom bracket: The component of the bicycle consisting of the axle and bearings on which the cranks turn.

buff: Fast, hard-packed singletrack. Also, a light beige color—not unlike the color of much fast, hard-packed singletrack.

bunny hop: (*n., v.*) The act of lifting both wheels above the ground, without a ramp.

cairn: A trail marker, generally used where the trail's course is not visually obvious or where it will be obscured by snow, as at high altitude. Most often a pile of rocks.

camber: Describes the lateral slope of the riding surface. For instance, a trail that curves right but slopes downward from right to left is called "off-camber." Off-camber turns are the opposite of bermed turns (see **berm**).

case: (*v.*) A bad way to land a jump, on the top or front of the jump instead of the backside transition; often results in a bad crash. A term borrowed from motocross.

clean: (*v.*) To ride through a section without putting a foot down.

dab: To put a foot down, as opposed to "clean."

doubletrack: A route wide enough for two bicyclists side-by-side. May refer to four-wheel-drive trails or two singletrack trails that are adjacent to each other.

dualie: A cutesy term for a full-suspension mountain bike, or "dual-suspension."

endo: To crash by going over the handlebars; short for end-over-end. In the UK, "endo" is used to describe an intentional, controlled "nose-wheelie," or "stoppie."

epic: A particularly long, excellent off-road ride.

euphonium: A tiny tuba.

freeride: Not really sure. This term means different things to different people, but refers generally to the genre of mountain biking that involves bigger jumps and drops than can be negotiated safely on a cross-country bike.

granny gear: The smallest (easiest) gear available on the bike, accessed when the chain is on the largest cog in the back and the smallest chainring in the front.

hardtail: A bike with front suspension but no rear suspension.

igneous: (*adj.*) Used to describe rock formed from magma that has cooled and solidified.

krummholz: The stunted, twisted trees found at high altitude, near timber line.

labyrinth: Assembly of odd-shaped bones and vessels in the inner ear, which is critical for balance.

line: The path of the bike on the trail. In reality, there are two lines, one for each tire.

manual: Like a wheelie, but performed while coasting instead of pedaling.

mojo: Magic, voodoo.

pinch-flat: A puncture of the inner tube caused by its being pinched by the tire casing in a hard impact.

pogo: To bounce up and down on a suspension bike. Usually refers to unwanted motion caused by pedaling. Also, a cartoon possum.

pump: To push the front end of the bike into a berm or down the backside of a jump; results in an increase in speed without pedaling. Also, a device for putting air in a tire or shock absorber.

rigid: Without suspension.

singletrack: Trail wide enough for one hiker or bicyclist. An old railroad term.

spindle: Axle. Used to describe pedal axles and bottom bracket axles.

spud: Term of endearment applied to early Shimano SPD "clipless" pedals.

switchback: A 180-degree or "hairpin" turn, often on the side of a steep hill.

technical: Rocky or other conditions that make a section difficult to "clean."

travel: The amount of suspension available from a shock, generally expressed in millimeters.

two-niner: A mountain bike with "700c" wheels.

washboard: Surface condition characterized by a series of wave-like humps and valleys, occasionally severe. Also called "braking bumps."

yard sale: A type of crash that results in some of the rider's belongings being strewn about.

NOTES

Preface

1. Wu Ch'eng-ch'ing, nineteenth century, quoted in Douglas Wile, *Lost Tai-chi Classics from the Late Chi'ing Dynasty* (Albany, NY: State University of New York Press, 1996), p. 45.

Part I: Riding Bikes on Trails

1. Sandra Kessler, "Still King of the Hill," *Black Belt* (August 1994), p. 52.

2. Douglas Wile, *Lost Tai-chi Classics from the Late Chi'ing Dynasty*, p. 26. For more on the origins of Tai Chi Chuan and other martial arts, see Dr. Jwing-Ming Yang, *Tai Chi Chuan: Classical Yang Style* (Wolfeboro, NH: YMAA Publication Center, 1999), and Donn Draeger and Robert W. Smith, *Comprehensive Asian Fighting Arts* (New York: Kodansha International, 1980).

3. Wu Ch'eng-ch'ing, "Song of Sparring" and "Postscript," quoted in Douglas Wile, *Lost Tai-chi Classics from the Late Chi'ing Dynasty*, p. 45.

4. John Long and Craig Luebben, *Advanced Rock Climbing* (Guilford, CT: Globe Pequot Press, 1997), p. 123. Chris Fellows, *Total Skiing* (Champaign, IL: Human Kinetics, 2010), p. 164. Terry Caron, "Tips and Exercises for Improving Cross-Country Ski Technique," Bright Hub, August 31, 2010, www.brighthub.com/health/fitness/articles/85384.aspx. Martin Dugard, *In-Line Skating Made Easy* (Guilford, CT: Globe Pequot Press, 1996), p. 37. W. Timothy Gallwey, *The Inner Game of Tennis* (New York: Random House, 1974), p. 36. Hal Wissel, *Basketball: Steps to Success* (Champaign, IL: Human Kinetics, 2004), p. 66. "Bowling Tip 1—Relax Your Grip & Swing," Ten Pin Bowling Tips, accessed January 15, 2011, www.petermartens.com/bowling-tip-1-relax-your-grip-and-swing.html. Brian Preston, *Me, Chi and Bruce Lee* (Berkeley, CA: Blue Snake Books, 2009), p. 91. Jack London, "The Joys of the Surf-Rider," *The Pall Mall Magazine* 42 (July–December 1908), pp. 330–31.

5. Bob Bondurant, *Bob Bondurant on High Performance Driving* (Saint Paul, MN: Motorbooks International, 2003), p. 43. Keith Code, *A Twist of the Wrist, Volume II: The Basics of High Performance Motorcycle Riding* (Glendale, CA: Code Break, 1997), p. 48 (emphasis in the original). Bryan Nylander, quoted in *Dirt Rider's Motocross Riding Tips* (Saint Paul, MN: Motorbooks International, 2002), p. 103.

6. Grey Larsen, *The Essential Guide to Irish Flute and Tin Whistle* (Pacific, MO: Mel Bay Publications, 2006), p. 96. Carl Jones, *The Birth Partner Handbook* (Naperville, IL: Sourcebooks, 2010), p. 98: "*Help her stay relaxed.* This is your foremost task" (emphasis in the original).

7. Charles Warring, "What Keeps the Bicycler Upright?" *The Popular Science Monthly* 38 (November 1890–April 1891), pp. 766–75.

8. Henry Gray, *Anatomy, Descriptive and Surgical* (Philadelphia: The Running Press, 1974; originally published 1901), pp. 859–67.

9. Erik Bendix, "The Art of Alpine Skiing and the Alexander Technique," Art of Alpine Skiing. Accessed October 13, 2010. www.moving moment.com/ski/ArtofAlpineSkiing--article.htm.

10. Bernard Hinault and Claude Genzling, *Road Racing: Technique and Training* (Brattleboro, VT: Vitesse Press, 1986), p. 103.

11. W. Timothy Gallwey, *The Inner Game of Golf* (New York: Random House, 2009), p. 39.

12. Ned Overend with Ed Pavelka, *Mountain Bike Like a Champion* (Emmaus, PA: Rodale Press, 1999), p. 11. I don't mean to disparage Overend's advice, which is generally excellent.

13. Online advertisement, Pet Product Advisor, accessed January 12, 2011, www.petproductadvisor.com/store/mc/big-heads-toy.aspx.

14. For example, see "Bowling Tip 1—Relax Your Grip & Swing," Top Ten Bowling Tips, accessed January 15, 2011, www.petermartens.com/bowling-tip-1-relax-your-grip-and-swing.html.

15. Ned Overend with Ed Pavelka, *Mountain Bike Like a Champion*, p. 198. Bernard Hinault and Claude Genzling, *Road Racing: Technique and Training*, p. 103.

16. Interview with Geoff Kabush, *Mountain Bike Magazine* (September 2008), p. 48.

17. *Stedman's Medical Dictionary* (Baltimore: Lippincott, Williams and Wilkins, 2006).

18. "Bush: 'I'm the decider' on Rumsfeld," CNN online, April 18, 2006, http://articles.cnn.com/2006-04-18/politics/rumsfeld_1_secretary -rumsfeld-military-personnel-fine-job?_s=PM:POLITICS.

19. Chuang Tzu, Chinese philosopher of the third century BC, translated and quoted by Arthur Waley, *Three Ways of Thought in Ancient China* (Stanford, CA: Stanford University Press, 1982), p. 47.

20. Arthur Waley, *Three Ways of Thought in Ancient China,* p. 48.

21. See Steven Dunbar, Reiner Bosman, and Sander Nooij, "The Track of a Bicycle Back Tire," Mathematics Association of America, date unknown (after 1996), www.maa.org/pubs/mm_supplements/dunbar/ bt2.html.

22. Bernard Hinault and Claude Genzling, *Road Racing: Technique and Training,* pp. 102–3.

23. Levi Leipheimer, "Ask Levi: Which Cadence Is More Efficient for Mountain Biking," CoachLevi.com, October 7, 2009, http://coachlevi .com/mountain-biking/which-cadence-efficient-for-mountain -biking.

24. Bernard Hinault and Claude Genzling, *Road Racing: Technique and Training,* p. 97.

25. John Howard, *Dirt* (New York: Lyons Press, 1997), p. 44. To be fair, the statement is outdated, and Howard's ideas about climbing may have evolved substantially. Howard's 1985 speed record was achieved in the draft of a vehicle with a specially designed windscreen. For information on the record attempt, see John Howard with Peter Nye, *Pushing the Limits* (Waco, TX: WRS Publications, 1993).

26. Dave Wiens, "The Road to Leadville: A Powder Day!" *The Road to Leadville* (blog), August 3, 2010, https://ergonbike.wordpress.com/ category/wiens-world/page/2.

27. W. Timothy Gallwey, *The Inner Game of Tennis*, p. 21.

28. This analogy borrowed from John McPhee's *Basin and Range* (New York: Farrar Straus Giroux, 1981).

29. Halka Chronic, *Roadside Geology of Colorado* (Missoula, MT: Mountain Press Publishing, 1980), p. 96.

30. Sheldon Brown, "Bicycle Tires and Tubes," Sheldonbrown.com, accessed December 29, 2011, www.sheldonbrown.com/tires.html.

31. Maxxis website, accessed January 5, 2011, www.maxxis.com/Bicycle/ Technology.aspx.

32. John Templer estimates the energy cost of stair-climbing at 0.548 -1.12 kilocalories per meter of ascent, and the energy cost of ramp-walking at 0.8 - 3.0 kilocalories per meter. John Templer, *The Staircase* (Cambridge, MA: M.I.T. Press, 1995), p. 33.

33. Richard Haier, Sherif Karama, Leonard Leyba, and Rex Jung, "MRI assessment of cortical thickness and functional activity changes in adolescent girls following three months of practice on a visual-spatial task," BMC Research Notes, September 1, 2009, www.ncbi.nlm.nih .gov/pmc/articles/PMC2746806. The study's findings were oversimplified in typical fashion by the mainstream media: "Tetris 'could boost brain power'" (*The Telegraph*, September 2, 2009).

34. Homer, *The Odyssey*, translated by Samuel Butcher and Andrew Lang (New York: P. F. Collier and Son, 1909), p. 173.

35. Keith Code, *A Twist of the Wrist* (Los Angeles: Acrobat Books, 1983), p. 104 (emphasis added).

36. See Franco Impellizzeri and Samuele Marcora, "The Physiology of Mountain Biking," *Sports Medicine* (2007), pp. 59–71.

37. From the online abstract of Hamilton Lee, et al., "Physiological characteristics of successful mountain bikers and professional road cyclists," *Journal of Sports Science* (December 2002), pp. 1001–8, www.ncbi.nlm.nih.gov/pubmed/12477010.

38. For example, see: S. Baldesberger, et al., "Sinus node disease and arrhythmias in the long-term follow-up of former professional

cyclists," *European Heart Journal* (January 2008), pp. 71–78; full text available online at www.ncbi.nlm.nih.gov/pubmed/18065754. F. Ortega, et al., "Extreme mountain bike challenges may induce subclinical myocardial damage," *Journal of Sports Medicine and Physical Fitness* (September 2006), pp. 489–93.

39. Julia Rommelfanger, "Endurance athletes at high risk of developing major arrhythmias, including sudden death," *Heartwire*, August 14, 2003, www.theheart.org/article/243897.do.

40. For more than you ever wanted to know about Ted Bundy, see Ann Rule, *The Stranger Beside Me* (New York: Pocket Books, 2009).

41. Kelly Koltyn, "Analgesia following exercise: a review," *Sports Medicine* (February 2000), pp. 85–98. The study described by Koltyn is A. Pertovaara, et al., "The influence of exercise on dental pain thresholds and the release of stress hormones," *Physiology & Behavior* (1984), pp. 923–26.

42. Trailside meeting with Dave R., October 2010.

43. Strachborneo v. Arc Music, 357 F. Supp 1393 (S.D.N.Y. 1973), http://cip.law.ucla.edu/cases/case_Strachborneoarc.html.

44. Marlin MacKenzie, *Skiing: The Mind Game* (New York: Dell Publishing, 1993), p. 33.

45. See Robert Hurst, *The Art of Cycling* (Guilford, CT: Globe Pequot Press, 2007), pp. 158–65.

46. P. T. Kim, et al., "Mountain biking injuries requiring trauma center admission: a 10-year regional trauma system experience," *Trauma* (February 2006), pp. 312–18.

Part II: Logistics

1. See *USA Cycling Rule Book*, 2010 version, chapter 6, section 6D, "Feeding and Technical Assistance," USA Cycling, PDF, accessed November 5, 2011.

Part III: The Big Picture

1. The Outdoor Foundation, "2010 Outdoor Activities Participation Survey," 2010, pp. 34–39.

2. Christopher Papouchis, Francis Singer, and William Sloan, "Responses of Desert Bighorn Sheep to Increased Human Recreation," *The Journal of Wildlife Management* (July 2001), pp. 573–82. Papouchis, et al., noted that "hikers caused the most severe responses in desert bighorn sheep (animals fled in 61 percent of encounters), followed by vehicles (17 percent fled) and mountain bikers (6 percent fled), apparently because hikers were more likely to be in unpredictable locations and often directly approached sheep." Audrey Taylor and Richard Knight, "Wildlife Responses to Recreation and Associated Visitor Perceptions," *Ecological Applications* (August 2003), pp. 951–63. The authors noted no difference in wildlife response to bicyclists or hikers. Terry Heslin, "Are bicycles appropriate in National Wildlife Refuges?" National Trails Training Partnership, September 21, 2008, http://americantrails.org/resources/wildlife/BikeRefugeWild.html. The author remembered one natural area in California where "there was a visitor's center and a self-guided auto tour. Bird watchers were instructed . . . to stay in vehicles—because the critters don't recognize Dodge Caravans as predators, but pedestrians cause alarm and flight behavior." However, Heslin noted a significant disturbance to birds when biking through the area that did not occur when driving, and concluded that it was "not appropriate" to ride in that particular wildlife refuge.

3. On the effects of trampling of sensitive vegetation and soils: David Newsome, Susan Moore, and Ross Kingston Dowling, *Natural Area Tourism: Ecology, Impacts, and Management* (Buffalo, NY: Channel View Publications, 2002), pp. 90–91. On the effects on wildlife: Richard Knight and David Cole, "Wildlife Responses to Recreationists," in Richard Knight, *Wildlife and Recreationists: Coexistence Through Management and Research* (Washington, DC: Island Press, 1994), p. 56.

4. Randy Martin, "Optimizing trail grade: the key to creating sought-after trails," National Trails Training Partnership, February 1, 2009, www.americantrails.org/resources/trailbuilding/MartinGrade09.html.

5. John P. Wilson and Joseph P. Seney, "Erosional Impact of Hikers, Horses, Motorcycles, and Off-Road Bicycles on Mountain Trails in Montana," *Mountain Research and Development* 14, no. 1 (1994), pp. 77–88. After experimentation on 108 sample plots along existing trails in Montana's Gallatin National Forest, the authors noted: "Multiple comparisons [sic] test results showed that horses and hikers (hooves and feet) made more sediment available than wheels (motorcycles and off-road bicycles) and that this effect was most pronounced on prewetted trails" (p. 77). Edon Thurston and Richard Reader, "Impact of Experimentally Applied Mountain Biking and Hiking on Vegetation and Soil of a Deciduous Forest," *Environmental Management* (March 2001), pp. 397–409. To view an abstract or purchase the full article: http://www.ncbi.nlm.gov/pubmed/11148765. Pickering, et al., "Comparing hiking, mountain biking and horse riding impacts on vegetation and soils in Australia and the United States of America," *Environmental Management* (January–February 2010), pp. 551–62. A good overview is Jason Lathrop, "The Ecological Impact of Mountain Biking: A Critical Literature Review," Wildlands CPR, June 29, 2003, www.wildlandscpr.org/ecological-impacts-mountain-biking-critical-literature-review.

6. "In streams and rivers, fine inorganic sediments, especially silts and clays, affect the habitat for macroinvertebrates and fish spawning, as well as fish rearing and feeding behavior. Larger sands and gravels can scour diatoms and bury invertebrates, whereas suspended sediment affects plant photosynthesis light availability and visual capacity of animals." U.S. Environmental Protection Agency, "What are Suspended and Bedded Sediments (SABS)?" accessed January 21, 2011, http://water.epa.gov/scitech/datait/tools/warsss/sabs.cfm.

7. Wilderness Act, 16 U.S.C. § 1131-1136 (1964) (emphasis added).

8. Theodore J. Stroll, "Congress's Intent in Banning Mechanical Transport in the Wilderness Act of 1964," *Penn State Environmental Law Review* (2004), pp. 463–65. Stroll quotes *Forest Service Manual*, United States Department of Agriculture Forest Service, 1990 (emphasis added). Note that wilderness areas are also managed by the Bureau of Land Management, the National Park Service, and the

Fish and Wildlife Service, but the Forest Service interpretation of the Wilderness Act is dominant in all respects.

9. *Ibid.*, p. 460.

Epilogue: The Window

1. Bliss Perry, ed., *The Heart of Emerson's Journals* (New York: Dover Publications, 1958), p. 155.

2. Lee McCormack with Brian Lopes, *Mastering Mountain Bike Skills* (Champaign, IL: Human Kinetics, 2005), p. 128.

3. Lee Bridgers, "Out of the Gene Pool and into the Food Chain," in Robert Rinehart and Synthia Sydnor, eds., *To the Extreme: Alternative Sports, Inside and Out* (Albany, NY: State University of New York Press, 2003), p. 186 (emphasis in the original).

Appendix A: Buying a Mountain Bike

1. Online question-and-answer session, Mountain Bike Forums, January 12, 2010, http://forums.mtbr.com/showthread.php?t=585008.

Appendix B: Two-Nine

1. Dave Wiens, *The Road to Leadville* (blog), July 7, 2010, http://ergon bike.wordpress.com/2010/07/07/marathon-championship-report -from-dave-wiens. In the comments Weins writes: "In my mind, the jury is still out, although JHK tells me he thinks his is a huge advantage."

INDEX

ACKNOWLEDGMENTS

Again I relied upon and pissed off a group of really nice folks while trying to write a book and work a regular job at the same time. Thanks especially to Christie. Also to Dave, Levon, Matt, Carlos, Steve, and Mike for dealing with the fallout. Thanks to my dad for helping out at a late hour, and to my brother for helping with some math issues. Thanks also to Scott Adams for endorsing the idea, and to John Burbidge for trusting the author, and dealing with the consequences.

Heartfelt thanks to all the riders who have taught me a thing or two over the decades. I have stolen your trail wisdom and made a book out of it. Thank you.

ABOUT THE AUTHOR

Robert Hurst is a Colorado native and a twenty-five-year student of the art of riding singletrack trails. He has also written *The Cyclist's Manifesto, The Art of Cycling* (formerly *The Art of Urban Cycling*), *Mountain Biking Colorado's San Juan Mountains, Road Biking Colorado's Front Range,* and *The Bicycle Commuter's Pocket Guide* (all FalconGuides).

Enjoy this read and want to learn more? FalconGuides has a book for all your favorite outdoor pursuits. Check out a few other great cycling titles:

The Advanced Cyclist's Training Manual

The Art of Cycling (formerly *The Art of Urban Cycling*)

The Bicycle Commuter's Pocket Guide

The Cycling Bible

The Cyclist's Manifesto

The Cyclist's Training Manual

The Evolution of American Bicycle Racing

Mountain Bike Maintenance

Road Bike Maintenance

Your next adventure begins here.

falcon.com